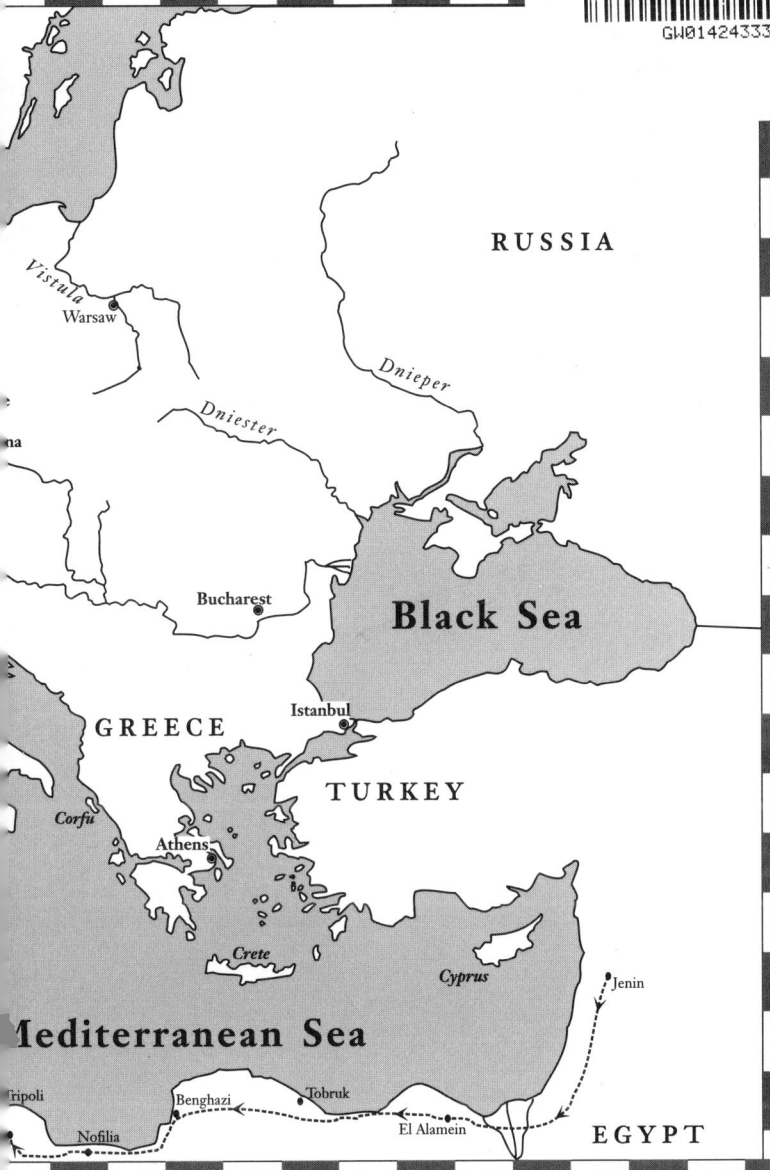

RUSSIA

Vistula

Warsaw

Dnieper

Dniester

na

Bucharest

Black Sea

GREECE

Istanbul

TURKEY

Corfu

Athens

Crete

Cyprus

Jenin

Mediterranean Sea

Tripoli

Benghazi

Tobruk

Nofilia

El Alamein

EGYPT

SWIFTER THAN EAGLES

Trooper Sprot, 1940

Second Lieutenant Sprot, 1941

Major Sprot, Coronation Procession, Edinburgh, 1953

Lieutenant Colonel Sprot, 1959

Swifter than Eagles

WAR MEMOIRS OF A YOUNG OFFICER 1939–45

BY LIEUTENANT COLONEL AIDAN SPROT MC

*'. . . swifter than eagles
to overtake thine enemies . . .'*

from the Regimental Collect
of The Royal Scots Greys

The Pentland Press
Edinburgh – Cambridge – Durham – USA

© A. M. Sprot, 1998

First published in 1998 by
The Pentland Press Ltd.
1 Hutton Close
South Church
Bishop Auckland
Durham

ISBN 1-85821-567-6

Typeset in Monotype Sabon 11/13

by Carnegie Publishing, 18 Maynard St, Preston
Printed and bound by Bookcraft Ltd, Bath

*This book is dedicated
to all those who served with me
in the War and who gave me the inspiration
to write it – and particularly to those who,
sadly, did not come home.*

Contents

PART III — NORTH-WEST EUROPE

Illustrations

Foreword
by
Field Marshal Lord Carver

Colonel Aidan Sprot's reminiscences of his service with the Royal Scots Greys paint a vivid picture of what it was like to be a young cavalry officer on active service in the Second World War. His regiment, later amalgamated with the 3rd Dragoon Guards to form the Royal Scots Dragoon Guards in 1971, was the last regular cavalry regiment, other than the mounted squadrons of the Household Cavalry, to be mechanized. Having enlisted as a Trooper and soon been commissioned as a Second Lieutenant, he joined the regiment in Palestine shortly before they were converted from horses to tanks in 1941.

Although they were late-comers to this new rôle, the Greys showed themselves as brave and skilful on tracks as they had been on horseback, when they first saw action in the desert shortly before the Battle of El Alamein in 1942. Their successful transformation owed a great deal to the firm and imaginative leadership of their commanding officer, Lieutenant Colonel Sir Ranulph Twistleton-Wykeham-Fiennes, referred to in the book as 'Colonel Lugs', who sadly died of a combination of wounds and sickness in Italy in November 1943. Aidan Sprot served with the regiment throughout the War, in which the regiment fought in North Africa, Italy and North-West Europe. I was fortunate to have them under my command in the 4th Armoured Brigade from Normandy until they met the Russians on the Baltic coast of Germany as the War ended. They never failed to perform every task with resolution, skill and élan.

Aidan Sprot's story shuns heroics and is told with modesty and restraint. It is illuminated by descriptions of the lighter side of wartime soldiering. The loss of comrades is mentioned with the stoic acceptance that it had to be at the time. It is therefore appropriate to recall that, of the approximately 500 men who were serving with the regiment at the outbreak of war or joined it later, 153 were killed or died of wounds or illness: 14 officers, 2 warrant officers, 33 non-commissioned officers and 104 troopers, as well as 2 men of the Royal Signals and 3 of the Royal Electrical and Mechanical Engineers attached to the regiment. While serving with the regiment in the field, 3 officers were awarded the Distinguished Service Order and 23 the Military Cross (two twice), one warrant officer the Distinguished Conduct Medal, and 15 sergeants (one twice), 2 corporals and 3 troopers the Military Medal. The pages which follow show beyond doubt that the regiment lived up to its motto 'Second to None'.

Preface

I wrote these war memoirs in 1947 more or less as they are in this book. I used three sources of information: firstly, the regimental war diaries; secondly, my own diaries which I kept for much of the War, in spite of it being against Army orders on account of security; and thirdly, my own memory which then was quite good.

My object of writing them was twofold. They give various routes of the Regiment in great detail so that this could be a fairly accurate appendage to Regimental history. And also, there were so many amusing, or sad, or typical, stories about individuals that I felt that they should be recorded for the interest of future generations. It must be remembered that all this was as seen through the eyes of a young regimental officer.

There may be incidents of which people have a different memory. If that is so, I apologize, but I have merely set down what were my own recollections. And if I have done a disservice to anyone then I apologize again.

Acknowledgements

Although I wrote these memoirs, more or less as they are now, in 1947, there are many who have helped me to get them, fifty years later, into this book form.

Firstly, I must thank that German typist-clerk in Ted Acres' Quartermaster's office at Lüneburg in Germany who, in the forties, deciphered my illegible writing and typed them. He has to remain anonymous as I have forgotten his name. Over a period of some thirty to forty years, I have added, subtracted, changed and corrected bits and pieces and Fiona Ballantyne, a neighbour in Innerleithen, retyped them – my gratitude to her – and to Major Tony Crease, Royal Scots Dragoon Guards, who had several copies made.

Friends in or connected with the Regiment who have encouraged me to publish them, my publishers – Pentland Press Limited – and especially Anthony Phillips, their Editorial Director and Mrs Mary Denton, Publishing Manager who have also encouraged and assisted me; Anne Couper, Peebles, who has done much typing of letters and bits of draft; my Regiment (now the Royal Scots Dragoon Guards) and especially Lieutenant Colonel Roger Binks and Major James Scott at Home Headquarters in Edinburgh Castle, who have found pictures and photographs suitable, and to Colonel George Stephen for his encouragement, fund of ideas and help in all aspects at all times and to Lady (Joyce) Brassey for permission to quote the poem in Chapter IV. To all these and to many others who, I hope, will forgive me if I have failed to mention them, to them all my most grateful thanks.

But most importantly do I thank all those I served with who gave me the impulse to record theirs and the Regiment's journey and happenings on the way from Palestine to the Baltic.

The book itself would never have taken off had Field Marshal Lord Carver GCB CBE DSO MC not written the foreword. Brigadier Mike, as we all knew him, took over command of 4th Armoured Brigade in the heat of the battle in Normandy after Brigadier John Currie was killed.

He was only twenty-nine and, as I hope I have brought out in the text, we thereafter had a Brigade Commander for the final ten months of the War in Europe whom we trusted implicitly and felt privileged to serve under. I am bold enough to think that this was reciprocated. Luckily for us he continued to command our Brigade in the first two years of peace and then again for a short period during the Regiment's next posting to Germany in 1959-60 when I was commanding. May I say a simple but most sincere 'Thank you, Brigadier Mike.'

Introduction

My father had been commissioned into the Royal Scots Greys and joined them in South Africa in 1902. Owing to commitments at home he retired after some five years and went on to the Reserve of Officers. He was then recalled in 1914, having twice been Adjutant to the Lothian & Border Horse. He was devoted to the Regiment; his study was full of regimental prints; he frequently wore the regimental tie and tweed and told me, as a child, endless stories of his soldiering. On his retiral from the Regiment he presented the Officers' Mess with the Cross-Country Challenge Trophy in the form of a silver heron – the family crest – the 'Sprot Cup', or 'Spro Po' as it is known.

So, having been brought up in this regimental aura, I was keen when I went to Stowe School to follow in his footsteps. However, he told me that was out of the question as I would need a personal allowance in a peacetime cavalry regiment and neither he nor I had any to spare.

Consequently, when I left school at seventeen, I was firmly sent to work in 'business'. I was in a bank in Edinburgh for six months and then in the City of London for two and a half years with the object of becoming an East Indian merchant. I did not like working or living in a city so I was relieved when war broke out.

I happened to be on holiday at home at the crucial time so, on the day after war was declared, I was taken by my father to Redford Cavalry Barracks where the 3rd (Horsed) Cavalry Training Regiment were stationed along with the 'Details' from the Regiment who had gone to Palestine in the autumn of 1938. Luckily we found Major Joe Dudgeon, the famous Irish showjumper, as second-in-command (an old friend of Father's in the Regiment) and the Adjutant was Captain Michael Borwick (son of 'Peach' Borwick, another of his regimental friends). I was recruited and my name was put down for the Regiment.

Some weeks later, I was called to a recruiting centre in Edinburgh for my medical examination and attestation, receiving the 'King's Shilling', but it was not till July 1940 that I was told to report to Redford

Cavalry Barracks as Trooper Sprot. There were some twenty PO's (potential officers) and we formed a squad for all the activities – stables, riding school, square, musketry and many others. The weather was kind and the two months there were reasonable and one got quite adept at changing one's uniform in the minimum of time. 'Bachelor buttons' were a great boon especially when all my tin fly buttons flew off as I was struggling into my 'pants, puttees and spurs' for the first time!

From here the PO's were sent to the Officer Cadet Training Unit (OCTU) at Weedon, the pre-war Army Equitation School. After one month here, the War Office sensibly realized that horses should not take part in modern warfare, so all horsed units at home were disbanded and our troop was sent to complete our cadet training at the Armoured OCTU at Blackdown.

Here we were bullied and chased unmercifully. Known as the 'Donkey Wallopers', they did not like us and invariably at reveillé our beds were turned upside down by the orderly sergeant to get us up! However, we took it all in good heart and I suppose maybe it did us good! In January 1941 we were commissioned in our various regiments and I joined other Greys officers who were attached to the Queen's Bays in Surrey and later near Marlborough, and who kindly looked after us very well till we got our posting order to the Regiment in Palestine in June.

Along with other subalterns in the Regiment – Bruce McLaren, who was rejoining, Matthew Arthur (later Lord Glenarthur), Dennis Fairhurst and Seymour Pears – we sailed from Avonmouth on 30 June 1941 in a small 12,000-ton Shaw Savill cruise ship – SS Mataroa – joining a large convoy with guardships somewhere off Ireland. There were about twenty young cavalry officers going out to join their regiments amongst a fair amount of others. Being small it was a friendly boat and we zig-zagged around the Atlantic for some three weeks till one morning I was woken by the watch shouting 'Land ahoy on the starboard beam'. Very exciting, this was Freetown, capital of Sierra Leone, where we spent two days in the natural harbour. We were not allowed off but many bumboats came out to sell their wares. I purchased a hank of bananas, out of which a few days later there emerged a large black tarantula spider which was disposed of by the steward, calmly saying, 'It will likely have its mate somewhere.' I continued to sleep on deck!

Another two weeks zig-zagging got us to Durban, with no sign of a U-Boat; we disembarked and were taken to a tented camp at Clarewood. We had ten enjoyable days here – a day's racing, a trip to Pietermaritzburg and, by an extraordinary coincidence, the South African officer I sat next to in the changing room after bathing in the sea at the Country Club turned out to be my cousin Billy Napier, whom I did not recognize as he had been out there for six or seven years. The remainder of my stay there was fun as he knew all the restaurants and night clubs!

Then we re-embarked on the Dutch super-liner, *Nieuw Amsterdam*, which had, I believe, held the Blue Riband of the Atlantic. As we prepared to sail, the famous 'Lady in White', in her wonderful prima donna voice, sang all sorts of patriotic songs and old favourites – very emotional but appreciated by everyone. The ship was capable of great speed and so was not required to sail in a convoy; her speed was much appreciated in the Red Sea as it produced a bit of a breeze.

When we landed at Suez we were taken to the Depôt at Abbassia for two nights and then onto the night train to Palestine. The Egypt/Palestine customs post was at Kantara on the Canal and great consternation was caused when they found Matthew's hunting horn in his case. On being asked what it was, he blew 'gone away' which caused even greater consternation!

We duly arrived at Tulkarm Station on 31 August 1941 and were collected that afternoon by the Regiment who were at Jenin. And so finally I was not only in the Greys but actually with them.

PART I — MIDDLE EAST

CHAPTER I

With the Regiment in Palestine and the Delta

The outbreak of war – 3 September 1939 – found the Royal Scots Greys in Palestine and still with their horses, where they had been for nearly a year helping to keep the peace between the Jew and the Arab. It was virtually active service for it entailed many small operations, mostly at night, capturing or killing leading Arab rebels. However, once the War began the two races appeared to forget their differences and, if they did not actually become friends, they at least ceased to fight each other on as big a scale as before.

During the first eighteen months of the War, therefore, the duties of the Regiment became fewer and many wondered whether it would not be better for it to be mechanized after all and do something to help win the War instead of sitting in a backwater such as Palestine. Consequently it was no very great surprise when the Regiment heard in May 1941 that it would lose its horses; but before being mechanized Regimental Headquarters (RHQ), Machine Gun (MG) Troop and A Squadron were to assist in the occupation of Syria as motorized infantry the following month. Major Dick Poole of the Rifle Brigade, who was soon known as 'Uncle', was sent to train this part of the Regiment with the help of some transport from the Trans-Jordanian Frontier Force.

The motorized part of the Regiment together with a motorized squadron of Staffordshire Yeomanry, the whole commanded by our own commanding officer Lieutenant Colonel G.H.N. Todd MC and called 'Todcol', left Jenin on 7 June for the concentration area and invaded Syria under the Australians by way of the Jewish border village of Metullah. 'Todcol' took part in an unpleasant battle at Merj Ayoun against very superior Vichy French forces equipped with tanks. Mirrlees Chassels's troop was surrounded and taken prisoner, Chas himself being wounded through the leg. These prisoners were returned after the Armistice but not before Sgt Binks had done a 'Cook's Tour' of the European capitals in a POW train. Cpl McGrath was luckier and passed back through the enemy lines with two others dressed up as Arab women.

On 19 July the Regiment officially became part of the Royal Armoured Corps and started to hand in troop horses to the Remount Depots, leaving only about twenty officers' chargers for recreation.

On 18 August 'Todcol' rejoined the Regiment having spent a short time at Suweida in the Jebel Druze after the Armistice; and three days later the Regiment received its first tanks in the shape of the three American General Stuart light tanks known as Honeys, on which mechanized training started in earnest, and it was at this moment that I joined the Regiment which was then stationed at Jenin.

✦ ✦ ✦

To train us into an Armoured Regiment from a horsed one in five months was no small matter but it was done, and this was because of the efforts of our 'Teacher', Lieutenant Davidson from 42nd Royal Tank Regiment, with half a dozen Sergeant Instructors. This training went on without ceasing till we left Palestine in February but everyone entered into it in the right spirit and soon became very efficient at his trade. As well as the three Stuart tanks we also had two pre-war British Mk IVBs. These had a crew of two and had no intercom so we used to tie string to the driver's arms and in true cavalry fashion guided him accordingly. When Roland Findlay[1] went for his first driving tuition in a Stuart with the instructor sitting on the driver's flap, the latter tried to slow him down by waving his hand, but Roland's reaction was to shout 'take your fucking hand away' and went even faster! In spite of SSM Clarkson, on being told that he could not have a truck because the pistons were out, exclaiming 'Hurry up and bring the truck, *mahleesh* the pistons' (*mahleesh* means 'never mind' in Arabic) and other similar episodes, the Regiment reckoned it was highly trained enough to take the field at the beginning of 1942.

While in Palestine at Jenin, we had a lot of fun, in spite of training hard to be converted from a mounted regiment to an armoured one. We had these twenty chargers which we frequently rode in the delightful

---

1   Major R.L. Findlay, Squadron Leader.

countryside, especially after the rains came and the whole place became a kaleidoscope of grass and wild flowers – jonquils, anenomes and cyclamen and many small and commoner ones. There was plenty of shooting – chikor and pigeons locally, and periodically we went to Lake Hule, in the top reaches of the River Jordan. This was an enormous area of swamp where geese, duck and snipe abounded. We would spend the weekend in the small Jewish village of Metullah on the Lebanese border at a good little boarding house run by the Lishansky family and go down to Lake Hule each day.

Jerusalem was often visited where there were good restaurants and hotels. The shops in the souk in the old city were fascinating – each street being of all one trade. The Biblical sites there were of great interest, as they were in other parts of the Holy Land. When I wrote home, I used to ask the Padre where those places I had recently been to were mentioned in the Bible. I would then quote chapter and verse at the top of my letter, hoping that my parents would realize why – and not think I was becoming a religious maniac!

Luckily my job was to teach soldiers how to drive. Out of some five hundred in the regiment, barely fifty had ever driven a car, these being mostly officers' servants and the one or two drivers in Motor Transport (MT) Troop. We used to take our haversack rations for midday, pick an orange or two or a bunch of grapes and go all over the north of Palestine, visiting every Biblical and archaeological site that I could find.

Occasionally we had a regimental concert in the open outdoor cinema. This was always excellently compered by Sgt Harvey Naylor and often had Frank Bowlby singing 'Old Father Thames' and Cpl Reddihough, the Post Corporal, singing 'Ave Maria'. One evening half-way through a concert, there was a crash behind the scenes and Sgt Naylor came on stage and, with a worried look, asked if there was a doctor present. Basil Miles, our Medical Officer, leapt to his feet, only to be asked if he was enjoying the show – he fell for it!

On 18 February the Regiment left by train from Hadera Station and by midday on the 19th arrived, after a most uncomfortable journey, at Khatatba, on the western edge of the Delta halfway between Cairo and Alexandria. The camp was a tented one sufficient for the whole of 8th Armoured Brigade and in the desert about a mile from the Delta itself. Our time here was spent in getting used to the desert by doing schemes round Bir Victoria, sometimes for the day, sometimes spending nights out. The Brigade was soon given some heavy Grant tanks and the first day they arrived, Colonel 'Flash' Kellet of the Sherwood Rangers was taken for a ride in his and was bumped into by one of our light Honey tanks, which suffered no damage but succeeded in putting the heavy tank off the road for several days!

To get to civilization – Cairo or Alexandria – you had to go via the 'Barrage', where there was a marvellous display of flowers, and through the Delta, or else take a bearing across the desert to the Cairo–Alexandria road. There was a line of barrels which took one to Km 42 but we soon got to know the way and could get far nearer Mena than that. Many were the times however that some of us got lost in the early hours returning from Cairo.

It was on this bit of desert that Peter Downie[1] and Bob Gregory,[2] the Technical Adjutant, wrote off a chaplain. They were going to Cairo and had Padre Ferrie in the back when they went over a big bump, threw him up and he landed on his ankle which broke. This put him into hospital and caused his place to be taken by Padre Maclennan, 'Tom Thumb' to most of us. He became our Padre for the next four years and was loved and respected by all. His arrival in the Regiment was comical. He appeared before lunch and came into the mess tent where he met Frank Bowlby,[3] Hugh Brassey[4] and John Warrender,[5] all over 6ft 3ins. They were soon joined by Colonel Lugs Fiennes,[6] Humphrey Guinness[7] and Roland Findlay, also that height. Wee Mac just came up to their elbows so they all thought it would be kinder if they sat. The Padre, with a glass of orange squash the size of himself, sat in a very soft armchair and consequently his head disappeared below the level of the arms! However, in spite of this rather shattering arrival in

---

1 Captain Peter Downie, Light Aid Detachment (LAD) officer attached to the Regiment.
2 Captain R. Gregory, Technical Adjutant.
3 Captain F.E.S. Bowlby, Adjutant.
4 Captain H.T. Brassey, Squadron Second in Command (2i/c).
5 Lieutenant The Hon. J.R. Warrender, Troop Leader.
6 Lieutenant Colonel Sir Ranulph Twistleton-Wykeham-Fiennes Bart., Commanding Officer.
7 Major H.P. Guinness, Squadron Leader.

the Regiment, he soon got settled down and lived as one of us from then onwards.

We were reasonably comfortable in our camp. The Mess was a double marquee with a concrete floor which made a great difference. Our sleeping tents were EPIP pattern which were not bad with three or even four of us in them; there was a Shafto cinema, built of carpets hanging on scaffolding, which was very satisfactory till one day it caught fire!

There was one real discomfort there which happened every evening and that was the wind getting up and blowing sand, which had been ground to a fine powder by the traffic, everywhere. However, one eventually got more or less used to it until one day there was a freak storm. About teatime we saw this wall of dust-laden cloud approaching us from the West; in a mighty swirling hurricane it slowly passed over us, flattening the Sergeants' Mess and other tents on its way; then when it had got to the other side of Cairo, it turned round and came back in the same wild manner. After it passed, it was a lovely evening during which we were busy shovelling sand off our beds and everywhere else, and putting up tents. The next day we picked up a copy of Abbassia Garrison Orders. It is not possible to say whether they were blown there, a distance of some thirty miles, or if someone had brought them, but the former is a possibility.

We used to get away for as many weekends as possible for we realized that we would soon be in the Western Desert fighting. We were also allowed one period of four days leave and I decided to spend mine in June over my birthday at the leave camp at Sidi Bish near Alex.

CHAPTER II

The Desert!

O n 14 June 1942 I took the regimental leave party by train to the Brigade Leave Camp at Sidi Bish, where I found Peter Halswell[1] in his usual luxury, rather perturbed that his period as Commandant, which had just started, would come to an end as there was a strong rumour that the place would close down owing to the rate of the enemy advance in the desert.

Sure enough, when I woke up next morning I found that Peter had already left for Khatatba at four in the morning and we were all to follow as soon as transport arrived from the Regiment. Everyone was discussing the situation, making the atmosphere tense and slightly depressing. However, we were fortunate in having a bathe in the sea which refreshed us before our party, consisting of three officers and thirty other ranks started off for Khatatba in one 3-ton lorry.

On arrival we were told that the Brigade was moving up to the desert proper as the GHQ emergency reserve, within the next day or two. Everyone started to pack, collect tanks, deliver stores and carry out other tasks; I remember wondering what to pack and what to store where. I decided not to take any winter clothing, 'as surely I'll be back in the Delta by then!'

On the 16th, the tank party went off by train, and I followed the next day in the road party in charge of A Squadron vehicles. What a day to celebrate one's birthday; I almost forgot that it was. We left at 6 a.m. in a Divisional convoy. Shortly after passing 'Half-Way House', a thick mist appeared, doubtless from the Wadi Natrun on our left and we had to slow down as it was like a real London 'pea-souper'. It disappeared shortly before Mareopolis and there we saw the Colonel's tank 'AUX I' lying on its turret in the ditch, having slipped off its transporter. Everyone thought: 'Is it the first battle casualty?' A few miles further on, there was a C Squadron lorry looking very bashed in

---

1 Major W. Halswell, HQ Squadron Leader.

a ditch, having been charged by a civilian car doing 60 m.p.h. in the mist. The civilian was nearly killed but our men got away with it except for a small cut on Sergeant Rich's face. At Amaryha a long halt was made and everyone brewed up.

This halt was on top of the hill overlooking Lake Maryut – a pink coloured salt lake – and the green coastal strip which was separated from the blue Mediterranean by the glistening white sand dunes.

The next bit of the journey was along the coast road and the difference in atmosphere and vegetation to what we had been used to at Khatatba was amazing. There was a continual sea breeze and always some form of greenery – fig plantations, palm trees and vines growing up the side of Arab huts. It was the same the whole way to El Daba where we arrived at 7.30 p.m. having covered 192 miles – on the whole a very pleasant journey – the desert here looking a lot nicer than around Khatatba.

I woke up with a start the next morning to see Tpr Ford on his motorbike just about to run over my sleeping bag in the semi-light on his way round to wake everyone up! The convoy started off at 6.30 and went to Km 90 between Mersah Matruh and Sidi Barrani with one long halt at Qasaba. The desert here was covered with 'cabbage patches, gooseberry bushes, old boy' as Humphrey Guinness used to describe these small areas of scrub. In these we dispersed and started to brew when the order was passed round: 'Move back to Charing Cross.' This was the road junction where the track to Siwa turned off. Evidently someone had made a mistake and sent us 50 miles too far. The convoy formed up again ready to move when it was cancelled till the morning. We had only just started campaigning and weren't used to these orders, counter orders, and so on.

This night was the first of many which has attracted me so strongly to the desert. I lay in my fleabag before going to sleep gazing at the myriad stars above, with an occasional one shooting, and listening to the plovers calling, which they seemed to do all night. Although in the daytime the heat is great, at night it's a pleasure to get under three blankets.

I went off ahead of the rest of the party the next day so as to reconnoitre and mark out the new regimental area on the Siwa track a few miles south of Charing Cross. We were met there by the Divisional

Commander, General Alec Gatehouse, who told us that the Germans were still advancing and had invested Tobruk and there was precious little else besides the frontier wire between us and them.

The wheeled vehicles arrived during the morning and the tanks in the evening. The tank train had gone to the railhead at Mischefa where they off-loaded on 17 June and remained in that area until the 19th when they re-entrained and went back to join the remainder of the Regiment in the area which was to be its home for the next few days.

The first morning here, I had to get up early to show the Colonel round the area. One can imagine my flap when I woke up half an hour after I should have met him. Having thrown on my clothes, I rushed over to RHQ where to my intense relief I found that he had decided to wait till the mist cleared and had not realized that I was late!

Here everyone was made to carry out operational routine to get used to what turned out to be our mode of living for the next seven months. We brewed up, tried to swallow very hard and dry army biscuits, got up before sunrise for stand-to and other operational duties. But there were the bright moments: Sgt George, the Mess Sergeant, unearthed the coloured umbrellas and set them up over the tables where we could drink warm, fizzy lemonade out of very sticky bottles; bathing parties went down to Matruh where people discovered they couldn't wash with army soap in the sea. On the way there I passed some Bays who were withdrawing and thought us mad to bathe with the enemy so close. However it kept our spirits up, so surely it was the best thing to do.

The situation was getting worse – Tobruk captured, Siwa occupied, enemy across the frontier at all points – and Brigade soon got the order that every other formation was getting: withdraw. B vehicles left on 24 June and went across the desert to Mareopolis, while the tank party left late at night on the same day and proceeded across country to Garawla Station. Here it was learned that all tanks were to be handed over – Grants to TDR (Tank Delivery Regiment) and Stuarts to 4 CLY (4 County of London Yeomanry), many of whom knew nothing about these tanks. This was depressing news to the Regiment when it was so near at last to having a crack at the enemy. Everything was so disorganized at the time that Eighth Army told the Commanding Officer that the Regiment would have to hitch-hike to the Delta! However, the Greys couldn't possibly hitch-hike so a train was found and everyone got on it except Tim Readman[1] and Alec Lewis[2] who set off for Daba to get some beer and NAAFI supplies from the dump before it was destroyed. When they got back, the train had gone, much to their dismay. Luckily for them, the last train to run was due in shortly.

This and the other train were heavily bombed during the night and a very gallant act was carried out by Sgt McMeekin and Cpls Naylor and Chalmers who unhooked a burning wagon of flares and isolated it from the wagons on either side which contained high octane petrol, thus preventing the whole train going up.

I had left Charing Cross on 23 June and gone back with other Brigade representatives straight to Amaryha Transit Camp, many miles away. We left at midday and were told to get there by nightfall. The road and verges were an amazing sight – two lines of traffic going West and four lines going East. It moved slowly most of the time until the level crossing near Fuka where there was an ammunition train halted across it. I never thought until afterwards how lucky it was we never saw an enemy plane the whole day. To get back that night I had been going as fast as I could and cut in badly in front of a loaded tank transporter, which had to jam on its brakes suddenly with the result that the tank nearly went through the cabin. I got some nasty looks and I expect a few remarks as to my 'windiness'!

Mike Farquhar, Staffordshire Yeomanry, and I had a good meal at Daba NAAFI and arrived at Amaryha at 11 p.m. to find John Prideaux and Matthew Arthur from Brigade Headquarters waiting for us.

I spent the next few days marking out at least half a dozen areas for the Regiment. No sooner was one completed than we had to move to another area. The Colonel's tank, having been put on its tracks again, had gone by road to Mersah where someone who wasn't in the picture had said, 'Oh yes, the Greys have gone to Mareopolis. You'd better go back there,' which they had done. I had to tell them to turn round again and go back to TDR!

Trucks and small parties were arriving daily and by the 30th the whole Regiment had appeared. The wheeled convoy which came across

---

1 Major A.G.J. Readman, Squadron Leader.
2 Lieutenant A.W.D. Lewis, Regimental Intelligence Officer.

the desert had caused a great stir in Alex as a recce plane had reported it as an enemy column.

On 1 July Mo Williams[1] was sent up to 2nd Armoured Brigade in a hurry in the middle of the night, in connection with an idea that the Greys would be equipped with Stuart tanks and operate as a recce unit in the Qatara Depression. The remainder of 8th Armoured Brigade went to the Canal Zone for refitting while we were sent back to Khatatba to draw the Stuarts.

I took over RHQ troop from Mark Bodley[2] who was away with a poisoned arm, but luckily was allowed to mess with A Squadron as I was rather frightened in those days of Colonel Lugs and Frank with his moustache!

We occupied our old lines at Khatatba and things looked much the same except for there being no tents. The five days here we spent in collecting tanks, holding them for an hour or two and then handing them over to someone else. After this had been going on for some time, we at last got firm news that the Regiment would be equipped with one Stuart Squadron and two Grant or Lee Squadrons. One bright spot during all this was being able to borrow Tpr Missen from the Bays, who were in the area, to cut our hair. He used to work in Thomas's and cut several officers' hair before the War.

On 8 July the Regiment moved back to Mareopolis with B Squadron fully equipped with sixteen Stuart tanks. The remainder of that day, the night and the next day were spent in drawing new Grants & Lees for RHQ, A & C Squadrons. B Squadron reported to HQ XXX Corps at El Hammam that morning and RHQ and A Squadron followed later in the day. C Squadron remained behind but were later attached to the 9th Lancers before joining the Regiment a few days later.

---

1 Captain Sir Michael O. Williams Bart., Squadron 2i/c.
2 Lieutenant M.R. Bodley, Troop Leader.

CHAPTER III

On the Alamein Line

I have gone into a fair amount of detail in Chapter II because it covered an interesting period, being the Regiment's first month after being mobilized as an Armoured Regiment. It travelled many miles, was moved around from one place to another yet never had a proper job and never even smelt the enemy.

From now on, the Regiment had a fixed role, although in the three months on the Alamein Line it was under the command of every corps and division of all nationalities.

✴ ✴ ✴

The next few days were spent under the command of 22nd Armoured Brigade with B Squadron forward observing from Ruweisat Ridge while the remainder of the Regiment was at Alam Baoshaza, centred round a very small depression, christened by Colonel Lugs 'the fishpond'. It was here that I experienced my first shelling. Luckily I was in my tank whereas Humphrey and Frank were outside theirs; I've never seen two people dive so fast before! These two were on the same tank – Humphrey rear link with Frank as operator – and many a time did Humphrey jump in in a bit of a hurry and land on Frank's head! An unfortunate thing happened to them here the evening we were going to the Alamein Box to come under the South Africans. Frank was sitting on top of the turret covered in maps, signal forms, attaché cases, earphones etc., and Tpr 'Duggie' Evans was filling the tank with petrol when 'woomph' and a sheet of flame shot up from the clutch shaft. Frank having disentangled himself from his earphones leapt off and got every one away. Luckily I was beside the tank when it happened and managed to pull the fire extinguishers but they made no difference. The flames got more of a hold and poor Humphrey and Frank watched their belongings burning inside including a lovely Canadian fur coat which Colonel Lugs had given Frank at his wedding. Shortly after, we were all sitting around 'Aux' at a conference lit up by the flames about eighty yards away, when there was an almighty explosion and the tank blew up, the turret sailing through the air and landing beside us. That was enough, so we moved off straight away as it was a perfect target to any Hun planes.

Our route to the South Africans was back by the desert to El Imayid Station, then up again alongside the coast road. We stopped that night before getting to Imayid and got to the station for breakfast and most of the day. It is an extraordinary thing that anywhere along the main road, as soon as you stop, you are besieged by Bedouins saying 'Eggis for chaay' (eggs for tea); so that day we fed well. We all had to lend poor Frank various shaving and washing utensils.

Before moving from here the tanks went to the shore and 'fired in' their guns out to sea. The new RHQ tank had just arrived and Colonel Lugs was very annoyed when no shell would go right home into the breech, but even more so when he discovered the cause was that the barrel was still packed tight with grease!

We had only been with the South Africans two days when previous orders were cancelled and we had to retrace our steps to 22nd Armoured Brigade. After a night at the 'fishpond' the Regiment moved south of Alam Nayl – or more familiarly 'Point 93' – which was landmarked by a burnt-out Grant which had received a direct hit inside the turret from a shell. It was on the way here that we suddenly met Colonel Charles Sismay (60th Rifles) commanding August Column whom we were to see a lot more of later. He was an old friend of Colonel Lugs and Frank's; it is extraordinary how you continually bump into old acquaintances in the middle of the desert!

Shortly after arriving here, Ollie Berger's[1] tank became our first battle casualty on a mine and thus formed a regimental code name ever since – 'Ollie's eggs'.

During the Regiment's first engagement with the enemy in front of 'Stuka Valley', Peter Ebrington,[2] after a very courageous advance through an enemy minefield, ran into trouble and lost two tanks. It was not then known what had happened to the crews but it has since

---

1 Lieutenant O.C. Berger, Troop Leader.
2 Lieutenant Viscount Ebrington, Troop Leader.

transpired that Peter was killed probably after dismounting. Rupert Milburn,[1] after dark that night, went out by himself, unbeknown to anyone, to investigate these tanks. He found no sign of the crews but the wireless was still working in one.

Another action in the same area a few days later resulted in Charlie Radclyffe's[2] tank being hit and he was severely burnt. This was a bad day for the officers for later Roland's foot was shattered by a splinter and Guy Holland[3] got shrapnel in his leg. Roland became the best-known patient in the Middle East hospitals and it was said to have been due to his tremendous courage and humour in hospital that many seriously wounded people pulled through.

The Regiment's next location was beside the 'North-South track', being a stone-bordered track running from El Alamein to Moghra in the Qatara Depression. It was near here in a depression that one of those fantastic lone palm trees stands. They appear so seldom that they are marked on maps and are a helpful guide in navigation.

C Squadron arrived back here from the Delta having got new tanks. Massey[4] had very proudly purchased some new bush shirts and came up to Colonel Lugs to show them off. That was the last time he ever wore them! I think that Jackie Pert, his batman and jeep driver, used them as dusters after that!

On 1 August the Regiment changed to 7th Motor Brigade and moved across to 'Bare Ridge' beside Qabr Hani Sada – one of those lonely Sheik's tombs. On the way Tony Cayzer's[5] tank caught fire and eventually blew up. Colonel Lugs and I were in a jeep and it was pitch dark, so I didn't feel too happy when he told me to take him to 22nd Armoured Brigade HQ to report it. We only had a four-figure map reference of Brigade HQ so I took a bearing to the middle of the square, lined up the jeep, picked on a star and set off; after about the right distance I thought I had better check up, so lying down I saw the silhouette of a truck against the horizon. I went over to it and asked if they had any idea where 22nd Armoured Brigade were. To my relief

---

1   Lieutenant R.L.E. Milburn, Troop Leader.
2   Lieutenant C.R. Radclyffe, Troop Leader.
3   Lieutenant G.R. Holland, Troop Leader.
4   Major Lord Roborough, Squadron Leader.
5   Lieutenant The Hon. M.A.R. Cayzer, Troop Leader.

A 'General Stuart' light tank near Himiemet

someone said I was in the leaguer and the Armoured Command Vehicle (ACV) was only fifty yards away!

Colonel Lugs was always full of practical ideas and at this time he thought out the establishment and tactics for a novel unit which would travel in jeeps and have some form of hollow-charge anti-tank weapon fitted on the bonnet. His idea was to have sections of three jeeps and, in a tank battle, these jeeps would be unleashed; then each section singling out an enemy tank would rush at it from different directions, and he reckoned that each one would knock out its tank at the cost of one or perhaps two jeeps. He wrote quite a screed and forwarded it through Brigade to General Horrocks, the Corps Commander, who acknowledged it. It would have been interesting to have seen whether it would have been successful if put into action.

It was generally agreed that the next three weeks in this position under 7th Motor Brigade were some of the happiest spent in the desert. The view from our position on the south face of Bare Ridge was perhaps the most striking in the area. In the foreground was Deir Muhafid; behind that from the left to right were the following features: Somaket Goballa (christened 'Sir Market and Lady Goballa' by Hugh!), low and rugged; behind it Qaret Somara; next the mass of Quarat Humur with the long hill, Qor Laban, behind; then Himiemet tailing off into the Taqa Plateau. All these somehow had a personality of their own and seemed to grow on one. Frank and I both likened Himiemet to the Eildon Hills.

The first day we were here we were visited by General Renton, the one-armed commander of 7th Armoured Division. He was very interested in the Regiment as his father had served in it many years ago. He walked round all the tanks taking a great interest in the men's welfare and made his Colonel A/Q take down verbatim Trooper 'Flash' Connel's remarks about the mouldy bread!

Forming leaguer one night here, Massey got into a bit of a muddle. Astra, the regimental intelligence officer's tank, had just been fitted at the rear with a red and green light and when forming up for leaguer it used to go in the centre and squadrons would come in on either side. Suddenly we saw Massey with his squadron arriving from the front instead of the rear. When he said 'Am I alwight here Colonel? I've followed the wed light,' the Colonel nearly blew up. It transpired that the 'wed light' was the wireless one which he had seen through the driver's hatch. Massey could not pronounce his Rs.

Every day here was spent in either firing on a range below Quaret Humur or recceing and practising occupying battle positions on Bare Ridge. We also went back to recce positions to withdraw to in the event of an enemy attack. These were code-named 'Pheasant' and 'Partridge' and were en route to the Delta. In the evenings squadron sing-songs were held after stand-to, to the accompaniment of an accordion – a very popular form of entertainment.

I used to go to the ranges every day with Colonel Lugs in the jeep and although we went the same way each day, there was always something new to see – a hoopoe flying about on Humur or a large iguana in Deir Ragil, etc. Some people visualize the desert as being dead but if you keep your eyes and ears open there is always something new in the way of a view, flowers, birds and other interesting sights. Shortly before descending the escarpment north of Humur, we met two Arabs and a donkey making their way from Moghra to Hammam – the first time I had seen locals so far in the desert near the front. We had eggs for breakfast for several days after that! At Moghra there is a local type of egg incubation hut. The eggs are spread out on the floor and the temperature controlled by the windows. It evidently is highly successful, but being naturally heated by the sun it would never work at home.

The weather ever since we came to the desert in July was perfect – very cold at night, very hot by day but always a cool sea breeze. Going out in the jeep at stand-to I always wore my old sheepskin coat till the sun came up when it started to get warm. We had one very bad Khamsin (a hot south wind off the desert), and I remember coming back from the ranges by Himiemet and the January minefield, with Colonel Lugs feeling very drowsy in front. He nodded off several times and nearly fell out, so he made me tie a rifle sling across the doorway to keep him in!

Seven o'clock one morning when we were peacefully shaving and breakfasting, Brigade sent one word – 'Economize' – over the air. This meant 'take up battle positions' which was quickly done. At midday it was learnt that this was due to an attack by a German infantry regiment against the New Zealand box, with no effect.

During this period we worked with the three columns of 7th Motor Brigade – 'March' , 'July', and 'August' – being composed of 60th Rifles, the Rifle Brigade and 3 RHA. Our battery was 'M' commanded by Terrence O'Brien Butler, another old friend of the Colonel. Colonel Vic Turner, of the Rifle Brigade commanded one and it was later with this column that he won his VC. I remember the first time I met him when his Battalion HQ was in Deir Munassib and he was having a very excellent breakfast in his staff car at the foot of the escarpment near where the sides of the depression almost joined and which he had christened 'the Narrows', obviously in memory of some bygone yachting trip. 7th Motor Brigade was a large happy family. The 60th, Rifle Brigade, RHA and Greys worked so well together that they might have been squadrons of one Regiment. Many officers of each Regiment were old acquaintances and used to go to each other's vehicles for a drink in the evening. Dick Wood of the 60th was attached to us for a while with his anti-tank platoon and lived with RHQ. It was very pleasant having him, and we were all very sorry to hear that during the fighting near Sirte at the end of the year he lost both legs when a bomb landed on them but luckily did not explode!

On 20 August, we moved to rejoin 22nd Armoured Brigade below Alam Halfa at a small feature commonly known as the 'Sausage'. While recceing this place we put up two gazelle – unfortunately we were not armed. As soon as we arrived, we had to clean and polish ourselves up to meet Winston Churchill and General Sir Alan Brooke (CIGS) on Pt 102 beside the New Zealand cemetery. Churchill looked a very tired man there and he apologized for not getting up when shaking hands with us.

As the moon grew old so did the expectation of the coming German attack which was probable on 26 August. A large-scale Army Exercise was carried out, the 'enemy' doing what it believed the Germans would do when they attacked. The 26th passed and no sign. Saturday 29 August saw several officer changes and Tim Readman became second in command in place of Humphrey who went to 'Reesforce'; Timmie Parker[1] took over as Signals Officer from John Gunn.[2] Sunday was very peaceful with a church service in a wadi in the morning and an Officers v Other Ranks baseball match in the afternoon. This peaceful time turned out to be the lull before the storm.

---

1 Lieutenant T.B. Fitzgeorge Parker.
2 Captain H.J.D. Gunn, Squadron 2i/c.

CHAPTER IV

Rommel's last bid

At about half past two in the morning of 31 August I woke up to hear Frank saying something about 'Twelve bore' to Colonel Lugs. In my semi-comatose condition I thought they were discussing the opening partridge shoot for the next day; then it suddenly dawned on me that 'Twelve bore' was the code name meaning the enemy had attacked. I jumped up, dressed, ran over to Tim's Honey tank and fired the alarm – three burst from his anti-aircraft Browning gun – then got Regimental Headquarters (RHQ) organized. The whole Regiment moved off to their battle positions which they had practised only a few days previously. From RHQ, on the side of the main feature, we had a real 'front row of the circle' view of the battle. You could see the enemy vehicles advancing across the plain between Deir Muhafid and Deir Ragil. Later in the afternoon, the enemy tanks turned north against the so-called Alam Halfa fortress where 4 County of London Yeomanry took the brunt of the attack and lost a squadron. The Colonel was then ordered to send A and C Squadrons from their positions in the west to fill the gap between 4 CLY and 5 RTR (Royal Tank Regiment).

> We went like hell in a cloud of dust,
> which swallowed the host of tanks,
> and the engines roared as if they'd bust
> as the Squadrons closed their ranks.
>
> None got a glimmer the way we went
> but none had a notion to stop,
> and we took the bank as we came – hell bent –
> like a fence with a five-foot drop.
>
> Out of the sun we rumbled past
> and arrived like bolt from the blue,
> and the RB's cheered as they saw us past
> In a Mechanized Waterloo!
>
> (Point 102 – Odd Odes by H. T. Brassey)

RHQ came with them and I was stuck down in the turret of the Colonel's tank as his gunner and could not see much through the periscope. When we halted behind the 'Island' I attempted to traverse a bit to see what was going on but only got a hit on the head and told to keep still! So all I saw were tracers flashing past the periscope. At last light, having lost at least twenty tanks, the enemy retired into Deir Dayis – christened 'Dan's face', because on the map it was represented by a lot of dots, reminding Colonel Lugs of the stubble on the face of Dan Mckergow who had served with the Regiment some time before. Our casualties were negligible. That night we leaguered at the back of the 'Island' and I was sent off on foot to Brigade HQ which was only a mile away beside the telegraph lines. Could I find them in the pitch black? I felt sure I should walk straight into the leaguer or anyway see the telegraph poles, but it was so dark I saw nothing. After going around for a bit I saw a cigarette burning which luckily turned out to be Brigade. It shows how easily a cigarette gives your position away. It was an unpleasant night as the enemy were continually shooting Verey lights and you could hear their tanks moving about.

However next morning the position was the same: later the enemy had another crack against 8th Armoured Brigade who had just arrived to the east of us. From now on the general direction of the enemy was to the west – their last bid for the Delta beaten. The Gunners and some of our tanks had some good shooting during the next few days at enemy transport and other targets on the plain below. B Squadron was sent forward to follow up and observe the retreating enemy. They had four very unpleasant days of watching, with much shelling and returned to the Regiment on 9 September. Then followed a week of reorganizing and several officer changes – Frank took over B Squadron, Rupert became Adjutant and Mark Bodley returning from hospital went to Brigade as LO.

It was on this plateau where RHQ was that we met a truck whose driver asked us the way to a certain unit. He said that he had been told to go the top of the plateau and turn left. The Colonel asked him, 'And I'm sure they told you that you couldn't miss them.'

He replied, 'As a matter of fact, Sir, they did.' A lot of people were as vague as that in the desert.

On 16 September the Regiment moved to the southernmost limit of the line under 4th Light Armoured Brigade.

CHAPTER V

Marking Time for the Great Offensive

In this area, the Regiment was the southernmost unit on the Alamein Line, and was situated among the familiar features we had seen on the horizon when on Bare Ridge. RHQ nestled under the southern slope of Humur, with B Squadron forward on Qor Laban. Seymour's[1] troop was on the south end of it affording a magnificent view over the Qatara Depression, which lay like a carpet below one – Moghra Oasis like a green smudge and the inevitable line of telegraph poles from Siwa stretching back. B Squadron HQ was at the north end on a feature which Frank called the 'pulpit' from the top of which they got a good view of Himiemet which was then in enemy hands. I often used to climb to the top of Humur in the evening and sit and admire the marvellous all-round view, especially the sunset behind Himiemet and Taqa.

To get to RHQ from the rear, one had to go through a sea of soft sand and only jeeps and tanks could make it. When the Colonel returned from leave he couldn't stand doing this the whole time so he settled on a new spot for RHQ beside some small boulders which reminded him of the rock gardens in Westbourne Grove, so that became its name!

On 23 September, the Regiment was relieved by 4/8 Hussars and went back to an area on 'Lady Goballa'. This feature covers a wide area and is in fact a plateau with fairly steep sides to the west and south and covered in small rocky hills and depressions. It was while we were here that General Horrocks, XIII Corps Commander, visited us and happened to ask the Colonel if he liked pipers. His reply was in the affirmative and he said he wished we had one on establishment. The General said that he would fix that. Nothing more was thought of it till Pipe Major Anderson of Aberdeen reported one day from the Gordons. He soon became one of the most popular members of the

---

[1] Lieutenant J.S. Pears, Troop Leader.

Regiment, waking us at reveille and playing most of the day. He stayed with us till a few days after the opening of the Alamein offensive when he grew so homesick reading of his fellow pipers 'going over the top' with the Jocks, that he was allowed to rejoin his Battalion.

Brigadier Mark Roddick, commanding 4th Light Armoured Brigade, had to go off on a big four-day exercise, and Colonel Lugs acted as Brigadier in his absence. He proposed to run the Regiment as well, as they were only about a mile away so I went with him as a sort of liaison officer. It was a pleasant break, Brigade HQ being situated in a small depression in 'her ladyship'. We ate at an officers' mess – the first time since June; the Colonel slept in the Brigadier's caravan and I slept under a lean-to outside it, using the caravan as a sitting room in the daytime. Here I learned the rudiments of staff work from George Dyer (11th Hussars) who was the GSOIII. They were a very nice staff: Joe Phillips, Brigade Major; Mick Baker-Baker, DAQMG; Mac Maclennan, Staff Captain; David Carmel, IO. On the way back to the Regiment one day I put up a covey of six chikor – desert partridge.

From here the Regiment supported 131 Brigade in a small operation to clear a part of the Munassib depression. A very difficult night approach march through some gaps in Nuts and May minefields with a following wind was carried out. David Callander[1] ran his tank onto a mine, and everyone thought the enemy would hear his curses! Tony Cayzer received a slight shrapnel wound in his head and had to be evacuated.

The wireless as usual provided a little bit of humour at a difficult point. Massey, along with his Squadron, was having quite a good shoot at the enemy guns etc. in the depression. He saw an enemy gun hidden in the wadi, so thinking that no one else had seen it, took his time laying his aim; just as he was about to say fire, someone else fired at it. He came up on the air with 'Some bugger's shooting at my fucking target!'

On 1 October we returned once again to 'Lady Goballa', but right at the forward or west end in a small depression. When you climbed up the rocky rim you could see right the way to Himiemet and the top of the Qatara escarpment. It was a very pleasant spot with a few small

---

1 Lieutenant J.D. Callander, Troop Leader.

flowers growing in crannies in the rocks. In the desert, one appreciates things like a moderate view, one or two small wild flowers etc. so much more than in a place where they are all taken for granted. It was here that Colonel Lugs said to me very seriously, 'What a perfectly lovely place' to which I agreed. Afterwards we thought how stupid people would think us at home if we raved over this barren patch of rock and sand.

The new Army Commander, General Montgomery, asked the Colonel to go to meet him while we were here. The Colonel, knowing Monty's eccentric idea of having the badge of every Regiment on his Rhodesian hat persuaded poor Tpr Prior, his servant, to give him his own treasured one to present to the General. I think the Colonel got a new one off Ted Acres[1] as he passed Echelon and so was able to give Prior back his!

We remained here till taking part in the great Alamein battle. Two large-scale exercises were carried out and, to put us off the scent, we were told there would be another one about 23 October.

On 17 October I went on my three day's leave to Cairo. Having had a whisky and soda in Has's tent, Bob Novotny[2] and I set off from B Echelon, with Padre Mac in his very bouncy truck. We went hell for leather in order to catch the Cairo train at Alex that afternoon. Our route was via 'C' track and when we arrived on the road at Burg El Arab, we looked like grey ghosts from the very fine powdered dust which blew in through the back. Once on the road Mac told Tpr Gibbard to 'step on it'. Very shortly a Military Policeman stepped out from behind a palm tree and stopped us – we had been exceeding the speed limit! Mac was furious and started to argue, his voice working up to a crescendo! We set off again with the threat that we would be reported! I missed my train so I had dinner that night at the Union Club (not Union Bar) and I was so out of training that half way through an exceedingly good and juicy tournedo, I could eat no more although there were still two courses to come!

I got on alright to Cairo the next day and there found David Callander. We had a terrific three days – most of it being spent at

---

1 Lieutenant (Quartermaster) E.J. Acres.
2 Captain Bob Novotny, Free Czech Forces, attached.

Shepheard's or Gezira. I suppose Cairo may be very boring for members of the 'Short Range Shepheards Group' who lived permanently there, but for one who arrived there for a couple of days from the desert, it was the last word in luxury and bliss and quite the most marvellous city that ever existed. Groppi, L'Hermitage du Turf, Dolly's, the Turf Club etc., were frequently visited. It was soon time for us to return so back we went by train to Alex and met Mac again. While he was at Alex he had done his usual commission for Peter Has which was to collect three thermoses full of iced Martini from the Cecil Bar. Can't you see Mac, only a bit over 5 foot, climbing on to a chair so as to see over the bar, then handing the thermoses over and asking for fifty (or whatever it was) iced Dry Martinis? Everyone was starting to stare but when he had finished arguing with the barman as to how many he had put in, he attracted the crowd from the gully-gully men, who were left without an audience!

Our journey back was quite eventful. I started off feeling very ill with a tummy ache after all our rich food and lay in the back of the truck not taking much notice of anything except that violent wind, sand and rainstorms were blowing up. We tried to make B Echelon that night but, realizing we were lost, stopped the truck in the dark in the middle of the desert and dossed down. You can imagine our horror when we woke up next morning to see a sign about twenty yards away, 'Corps Commander's Caravan'. We had stopped right in the middle of XIII Corps HQ on the top of Alam Halfa. We very soon moved, brewed up at a more discreet distance and arrived back feeling more tired and exhausted than we were when we set out! However, the leave, while it lasted, was worth a lot.

CHAPTER VI

The Battle of El Alamein

As October grew to a close everyone felt that the impending big offensive by us was getting closer and closer. It was a very well-kept secret until the morning of the 23rd when Colonel Lugs talked to Squadrons in turn and told them that the great day had come and the Eighth Army would attack that night. He gave a very impressive account of the Army's available equipment and what part the Regiment was going to take. The remainder of that day was spent in finishing off small details to the tanks, everyone feeling relieved that the storm was at last about to break, but also very quiet and meditative. New tanks kept arriving right up to H-Hour, to make us up to establishment.

H-Hour was 2130 hrs and the Regiment followed 44 Recce Regiment up to the first (January) minefield in two columns making for the two gaps to be cleared. In that approach march a carrier in the next-door column struck a mine, before arriving at the main minefield, and caught fire. Tim Readman, with his usual disregard for his own safety, ran across and helped pull out the wounded. It was a slow business, this march, but at the correct time the Recce troops arrived at the minefield with a Scorpion (flail tank) escorted by two B Squadron Stuarts. The whole time Colonel Lugs was in front standing up with Alec Lewis in the turretless Astra, directing operations. That night was a haze to me, at the rear of the tanks with the remainder of RHQ – shells bursting, tracer flying, small arms firing and other nasty things. When the 24th dawned, we were safely through the first minefield but had not reached the second (February). We had only a small bridgehead but it was slowly consolidated, again under the personal direction of Colonel Lugs who, during one of his recces, saw two Italians lying wounded away out in No Man's Land. He took Astra out to pick them up while all available enemy small arms were directed at him. He and Alec were lucky in that the only damage was a 20mm through a bogey wheel and a 5mm explosive bullet which hit the A/A gun and spattered their faces. Even during this exceedingly bloody battle, there was the usual bit of humour. In the pitch dark, except for the gun flashes, Frank came up on the air: 'Follow me. Can't you see me? I'm waving my flag.' The next day John Warrender was told to take his Stuart Troop back to refuel. I don't know if he was asleep or what but instead of going through the minefield gap, he went straight across the minefield and all three tanks were blown up. Poor John got out very gingerly, tiptoed to the gap and stood there looking very stupid, especially when he had to answer the Colonel's question, 'What has happened now?'

Basil Miles, our doctor, who had worked like a Trojan all night at the RAP came up to RHQ to see what was happening, and, while talking to Tim, was very badly wounded by a shell splinter in his stomach. I injected him with morphia and he was so helpful as he told us exactly which side to lie him on and how to bandage him.

This day and the next night were very unpleasant. Shells were dropping everywhere. We put on a brew behind the tank but before it was ready we had to move leaving tea, sugar, thermos etc. lying there, much to our rage. That evening the enemy put in a tank counter-attack when Sgt Hope, one of our best young tank commanders, was killed instantly when he was hit in the head by an AP (armour-piercing shot). Darkness came on and orders were received that the Brigade was going to attack February minefield with us in reserve. Rain and shells started to fall together and everyone really felt miserable. We were thankful when we were withdrawn the next morning to just east of January. While everyone was getting a wash, shave and brew, Italian planes dropped some bombs on the tanks. Alec got a nasty wound in the back which was to send him away till we got to Tripoli at the beginning of the following year. Massey, who was lying under his tank, had the tip of a breast shaved off by a bit of shrapnel and a piece entered his foot which gave no trouble till later when he had to go to hospital.

I took over as Regimental IO (RIO) from Alec, and that afternoon the Regiment undertook a small reconnaissance in force on the right flank. Some captured 4th Hussars came in, otherwise it was uneventful. That night, while everyone was having their first sleep for three nights, the leaguer was shelled. Tpr Bain, B Squadron, was killed, two more being wounded. I was sleeping beside Astra and got covered in sand from a very close shell. The remainder of the night we slept in the tanks.

On the 27th we were withdrawn east of June minefield for two days' maintenance. Great excitement was caused the first morning when a huge flock of cranes flew over fairly high, looking like geese. 'Johnny Blackpatch's' (John Barclay) Battery of Norfolk Yeomanry (anti-tank guns) – born and bred amongst the geese on the Norfolk Broads – opened up with all the small arms they possessed; this was taken up by the whole of the Greys. There was a veritable fusillade and not one came down, although we managed to separate one from the flock. This little interlude rather annoyed the higher-ups and the poor 4/8 Hussars who were next door to us, and had not fired a shot, got a very strong rocket!

I started to lose my appetite here, and this, with certain other signs, was the start of that dread disease so many were getting – jaundice. The very sight of food made me sick; in fact when I poured out my cup of tea one morning, the very noise of it going into the cup made me sick straight away. I stayed in bed most of that day eating nothing. Brigadier Mark Roddick came to talk to the Regiment about the operation and the future but as I was being carted off to hospital soon and felt very ill, I did not go.

The next morning I was bundled off, feeling rather that I was 'ratting' but I convinced myself I should be more of a hindrance staying while feeling so ill.

CHAPTER VII

Hospital

I was away from the Regiment for the next seven weeks. The jaundice made me feel so ill that I was thankful I was on my way to hospital, clean sheets and a bed. But when I felt better I longed to be back to take part in the pursuit.

The journey back to hospital was long and tiring. I went through the usual channels – Advanced Dressing Station (ADS), Main Dressing Station (MDS), Casualty Clearing Station (CCS) – each more grim than the last: stretchers coming and going: some corpses covered in blankets: doctors coming in and out with white overalls and masks on: people being sick: while I was lying on a stretcher preventing myself from being sick having had a sip of nasty sweet and weak tea. We arrived at the CCS about one in the morning and were met by none other than Johnnie Johnston who was on the staff there; he joined the Regiment a few days later as MO to replace Basil Miles. Next day we went on by ambulance to the railhead at Burg El Arab – not a bad journey, except the driver nearly got lost. Here we got on to a hospital train – very crowded and very stuffy; however we could lie down on the bunks and get a bit of sleep. At every large station which we stopped at in the Delta some kind Egyptian ladies (presumably members of their equivalent to our WVS) brought us tea, cakes, chocolate and cigarettes. Having not eaten for about five days, I suddenly had a violent hunger and devoured a mass of cakes which promptly make me sick!

I can't remember when we arrived at Qassassin Station, but we were taken by truck to No. 6 General Hospital and put to bed in the Officers' Medical Ward. I was a fortnight there and thoroughly enjoyed the rest. There was nothing very much to do so I took up knitting face flannels, and reading. Most of the ward were jaundice cases, and I had Colonel Guy Jackson, Warwickshire Yeomanry, in the next door bed. I never saw anyone so uncomfortable in bed. He had a very high temperature and was sweating fairly freely; whenever he tossed or turned his huge bulk, all his bedclothes came off; the night nurse was continually tucking him up!

We had good food here to start with: eggs, fish and chicken. But this was not to last as some new doctor arrived to say that eggs were bad for us, so we did not do so well after that. The best thing of the lot was the buffalo milk of which I drank a lot every day. When I got up after ten days, my legs felt just like macaroni but I managed to wander over to the washhouse – till then I had been shaved in luxury in bed by an Arab barber before breakfast. There was a very good canteen where we used to go and have a second evening meal, we were so hungry. I walked along to No. 4 Hospital next door and there found Massey hobbling along on sticks, the result of the small bit of shrapnel which had gone into his foot on 25 October.

We were told here that we should all go on to a convalescent depot for a fortnight, so I immediately applied to go to the one at Nathaniya or to Lady Macmichael's convalescent home in Jerusalem as I was longing to return once more to Palestine. My spirits fell when we were told that we were all going to the one near Ismalia on the Canal. We arrived at this very barren, godforsaken place, which made me even more depressed. Most people were wanting to stay here as they were near the cinemas etc. at Ismalia and Port Said. I went to the Orderly Room and asked what chances there were of getting to Palestine. I was told that some of us were being sent on to El Arish in Sinai and I could go there; so I thought that was better than nothing.

The next ten days I had at El Arish were some of the most enjoyable I've ever spent. It was a lovely situation right on the sea with a fringe of date palms in front, the old village behind with the hills away in the distance. The Mess was very comfortable and the Commandant was Colonel Sparrow RAMC, very keen on horses and an excellent artist. He used to look after cavalry officers very well as he had been ADMS to 1st Cavalry Division in Palestine.

I spent my time here exploring the village with all its quaint little shops – the silverware merchant, I remember best, sitting making very delicate bracelets; also the shop where we got Turkish delight. The Governor's residence – El Arish is the capital of Sinai – was a real oasis in this dusty village, with magnificent gardens in a blaze of colour laid out and carefully tended by Major Jarvis, one-time Governor who had written many books about this area. Most afternoons I went riding on the depot horses and to my delight found that the dates were just the right height to pick mounted. One day, two of us went deep-sea fishing in an Arab boat but caught nothing except seasickness. Gavin Astor, Life Guards, who was also convalescing, and I had tea with Colonel Sparrow one day and were shown his albums of drawings, photographs and cuttings, a very interesting collection. The bathwater system was none too good so we normally finished up the evening with a bathe.

The main Palestine railway line ran about ten yards in front of the building and whenever the one or two daily trains came along, all the local children would crowd round and put piastre pieces on the line, and keep the flattened-out coins for luck. The local Arabs were a mixture; you could see a few of the very fine-looking, swarthy Bedouin – the aristocrats of the desert – who would show up the scraggy and rather sloppy village men. The women all wore very heavy necklaces made out of old coins – the more coins the better off the wearer. While looking at the ruins of the old fort one day I met an Arab, claiming to be a hundred and seven years old. He certainly looked pretty old, but I doubt if he was that age.

I was very sad when I had to leave here and return to being a soldier again. I couldn't get a sleeper on the train so I laid out my valise in the corridor, having locked the door at one end. I slept very well till we had to cross over at Kantara, and didn't discover till afterwards that I had locked everyone away from one of the few lavatories on the train!

I spent three days at Abbassia waiting for a convoy going up to the desert. Luckily, I found Seymour Pears and Stanley Christopherson (Sherwood Rangers) there, also waiting.

We had a good fling in Cairo for the last time. Gezira and Shepheards will remain for many years in my memory. A perfect day from Abbassia was to go down to Shepheards about 11.30 in the morning and sit on the veranda with fresh lime drinks piled with powdered sugar. Then drift into the bar where Freddie, the barman, and 'Camelback' would serve us. The latter, an old Sudanese, earned his name when he went for a holiday, and, missing his train back to Cairo, returned on 'Camelback'! After a very good lunch, we would take a gharri to Gezira, where we would immediately change and plunge into the pool and remain there all afternoon, coming out about five o'clock for tea. I always tried to get a table in the faraway corner where you could watch the polo. A clap of hands and a shout of 'Ismah' would bring a waiter who would produce tea. A 'Rais' in his lovely green robe would wander round to ensure you had everything. After changing I used to stroll round the lovely grounds and watch any of the following sports: polo, golf, tennis, croquet, cricket, football (in season), squash or bowls. There is also a racecourse. The grounds were divided into three areas, each one being artificially flooded from the Nile for two days every week to keep the grass alive. About seven o'clock we would return to Shepheards and have a session in the bar with a lot of friends who were always found there. Then rather late and hungry we would go to the garden restaurant and have dinner outside watching the dancing. What better day could one spend!

One morning I set out to go to the Muski – the native market. I meant to go by myself and 'yella'ed' (told to go away) all the Dragomen. But I got so bothered by them that in the end I thought it better to take one, who got us a gharri and off we set. The Muski comprised many narrow walks with open shops either side. A wide variety of articles were all made in these shops and we watched craftsmen making brass pots and inlaid mother-of-pearl trays before visiting a fascinating shop where they made many kinds of jewellery out of all shades and types of amber. They were the agents for Aspreys, a fact which made the owner very proud. Our next visit was to a scent shop where the proprietor sat you down on a divan and produced coffee. Then he would bring in a huge cabinet of bottles, each a different perfume, and, mixing certain ones, would produce some lovely and some horrible scents. He also had some beautiful brocades for sale but they were phenomenally expensive. I would have liked to have stayed longer in the market but I had to go having bought an amber necklace and an inlaid mother-of-pearl tray.

On 8 December, we left Abbassia early in the morning with several lorries containing soldiers, including some Greys. There was a very unpleasant Lieutenant in charge of the lorries, who made a thorough nuisance of himself. Stanley, who was a Major, told him what he thought of him when we halted at Mareopolis. He gave us no trouble after that. It took us, I think, three days to get to a Tank Delivery Squadron (TDS) at Bomba, just beyond Tobruk. It was a pleasant, cool journey the whole way, and we managed to stop at various bulk NAAFIs to get beer, chocolate and other goodies. Mersah Matruh Transit Camp gave the best meal I've ever had from a similar establishment. Much to the annoyance of a small minority Tpr Sheil, a Grey and once a hunt servant, blew 'reveille' on my hunting horn every morning!

At Bomba we were told we would be kept till called for by the Regiment who were far too busy fighting to think about us. Seymour and I amused ourselves for two days, bathing and going for pleasant walks along the coast with all the wild flowers out. We then couldn't stand it any longer, and found out there were two armoured cars to be taken up to XXX Corps. He and I said we would drive them up and took Sheil and Leigh-Gilchrist as servants. We spent the first night in the cars in pelting rain near Derna Airfield. The next morning was fine but we couldn't get the Marmon Harrington to start, so we towed it to a RAF unit on Martuba aerodrome where they spent an hour or more tracing the fault, which was none other than the master switch being off! On we went through Derna, then into lovely Jebel country which was covered in trees and bushes, with the odd smart white Italian colony dotted about. The next night, having gone through the delightful large Italian village of Giovanni Berta, we stopped at a smaller one near Cyrene called Luigi di Savoia where the church had been turned into an ADS. The MO in charge directed us to two small, empty cottages where we stayed the night and were able to get a roaring fire going to dry our clothes. Carrying on after breakfast the next day we went through some more lovely scenery to Barce, where Seymour lost control of his Daimler going down the hill and ran into the back of a lorry which came off worse. That evening we reached the Advanced TDS north of Benghazi. By this time we had amassed a lot of rations, as, at every Field Maintainance Centre (FMC), we thought we would be another week on the road so we kept drawing a week's rations. We spent two days here while the TDS moved to Agedabia, then carried on to XXX Corps HQ at Wadi Matratin just beyond Marble Arch. It was 17 December by now, and we were some of the first up the main road as the Army had done another hook through the desert. At Corps we found about ten of our NCOs. We had to hand in our armoured cars here and were asked if we would take up ten jeeps to 4th Light

Armoured Brigade. Having this collection of NCOs we were able to, so we arrived back on 18 December with the Regiment at Nofilia and heard the sad news that Mark Bodley had been killed the day before when he and Colonel Lugs, who was badly wounded in the thigh, had led the Regiment in Astra in a charge against some anti-tank guns, which had got two direct hits on her.

CHAPTER VIII

Christmas at Nofilia, 1942

The first few days at Nofilia were spent in refighting the last battle and taking Tactical Exercises Without Troops (TEWTs) on it. There were several knocked-out tanks on the battleground including an OP's Honey tank, burnt out on top of a small hill which became known as 'Honey Hill'. It was on this hill that Duggie[1] had a unique experience. During the battle he went slowly up one side of it in his tank and saw the head of a German tank commander doing exactly the same thing the other side. They were only about twenty-five yards apart and neither could get far enough to fire his gun without being fired on himself. He tried firing delayed action HE, hoping it would bounce on the crest and burst over his opponent's head, but that did not work; he tried firing his tommy-gun held high above his head but his aim was too erratic, so after a few minutes, they said 'good afternoon', touched their caps to each other and departed.

During these days we all visited Mark's grave set in a small wadi. It was made very nice with shell cases, pebbles and a few wild flowers. I'm sure I could walk right up to it now, although the Imperial War Graves Commission could not find it; yet it may have got washed away in a flood or covered by drifting sand.[2]

On Christmas Eve the Brigade, less Greys, were ordered to follow up the enemy who were now retreating past Sirte. We were indeed lucky to be left alone for our first Christmas in the field. We came under command of 2nd NZ Division with that great General, Bernard

---

1 Major D.N. Stewart, Squadron Leader.
2 In 1954 when the Regiment was at Barce, we made an expedition to Nofilia to study the battle and look for Mark's grave. We found a grave and dug it up but it was a Bedouin's – they are buried on their side. However when we wrote to the War Graves Commission for a copy of the Regiment's burial report of December 1942 with a map reference and description so that we could have another search later, they replied very apologetically that they had eventually found it and had failed to tell us. He was reinterred in one of the main war cemeteries.

Freyberg VC, in command. The Christmas dinners had to be collected from Marble Arch over 100 miles distant, but it arrived just in time to be cooked. Christmas Day was very touching: a simple service with all the good carols taken by Mac on the hillside; men's dinners, clustered round the cook's wagons and attended by all officers who drank the usual toast – it is difficult to break tradition. Our own lunch under the tarpaulin which served as a mess was a large affair as about ten BBC and newspaper reporters had come to spend Christmas with us. They helped to publicize the Regiment by articles and broadcasts but they also helped to eat our meagre rations. Poor Johnnie Johnston had hoarded a tin of Australian peach jam which had been sent for Christmas. The reporters discovered this tin and finished it off to the refrain: 'What excellent ration jam you get!' Johnnie was very good and didn't say a word. After they had gone we discovered they had left their awful old knives, spoons and forks and taken our good ones. After lunch we all gathered round a wireless and there, in the middle of the desert, thousands of miles from home, dressed in all sorts of garbs, we stood at the salute while the Anthem was played before the King spoke. This scene was very nicely written up in an article in the *Egyptian Mail*.

Senior officers had changed quite a lot. Tim was commanding with Frank as Second in Command and Ru still Adjutant; squadron leaders were Duggie, Peter B[1] and Peter Paget[2] (Massey had been wounded and slightly burnt the same day as the Colonel). I became Regimental IO and Richard Shelley[3] Signals Officer. As RIO I arranged for another 'Astra' – a turretless Honey tank, ideal for navigating. My crew were Cpl Spencer as operator and Arthur Smith 25 (twin of Doug Smith 64 in C Squadron). Smith and I were to remain together till 1947 except for two short periods. He was of a charming family of farmers from near Kintore in Aberdeenshire, and I could not have wished for a better or nicer driver.

Hogmanay turned out like midsummer and Richard and I had quite a warm bathe in the sea. That evening there was a singsong in one of the wadis but the customary Sergeants' Mess smoker was not held for obvious reasons. The New Zealanders celebrated with tracers and

---

1 Major P.M. Borwick.
2 Major P.W. Paget.
3 Lieutenant R.R. Shelley.

King's Speech Heard By Men At Sirte

BY ERIC LLOYD WILLIAMS,
Reuter's special correspondent

OUTSIDE SIRTE, CHRISTMAS DAY. HUNDREDS OF RADIOS IN TANKS, IN TRUCKS AND TEMPORARY DUG-OUTS AMONG THE SAND-DUNES ALONG THE COASTAL BELT EAST OF SIRTE VILLAGE PICKED UP THE KING'S SPEECH TO-DAY AS THE EIGHTH ARMY CELEBRATED CHRISTMAS WITH NO FIGHTING OF ANY SORT.

Not even the occasional gun-fire which marks lull-time in the desert was heard to-day, and the only activity was the steady movement of the petrol, water, food and ammunition convoys to the front, and the long columns of guns and tanks moving through the desert into the Sirte area, ready for the next phase of the desert war.

Together with the Regimental Headquarters of a famous British tank regiment I heard the King's speech. We parked in a shallow wadi which twists southward through the sand-hills southward from the sea, and there were more than a hundred officers and men gathered round the radio, which had been set out on an empty petrol tin for the occasion.

The men gathered in a silent circle under a dismal sky to hear the speech, which came over very clearly on the set used for inter-communication work among the regiment.

Round The Fire

Some were wearing battle-dress alone, some British warms, some sheepskin coats, and all gathered near the fire which had been made in a petrol tin near a Sherman tank.

Next to me was a Czech officer who fought in Poland against the Germans. On the other side was a South African sapper with two New Zealanders and a Scottish sergeant.

«No word was spoken until the speech was completed, and then as «God Save The King» was played, every one came to attention and the officers saluted. After that everyone dispersed to their various tanks and trucks without speaking more than a few words. It was a truly impressive sight. I noticed a suspicion of tears in the eyes of more than one man.

To-day has been a very quiet Christmas indeed.

General Montgomery spent the day in his caravan headquarters of the Eighth Army, and not a single shot was fired by the forward troops. But all day and at night under the near-full moon the supply movement went on.

Along the coast road and south along the desert tracks guns moved forward, bouncing behind their tractors on the rough going, tanks clanked up among the sand-hills, moving into position and lorried infantry in the backs of trucks, most of them singing, went to their battle stations in the desert.—Reuter.

This article was written by one of the correspondents who lunched with us on Christmas Day 1942.

Listening to the King's Christmas Day Speech, Nofilia, 1942.

airbursts. This fine day was the start of one of the worst sandstorms that I experienced in the desert. There was a westerly gale, visibility was practically nil for three days, and the temperature was just on freezing. During this storm, General Montgomery paid a visit to the NZ Division which included ourselves. I was sent to the main road to guide him to our area. I arrived very early and was hanging about in my old fur coat in this awful storm when I saw an officer in an old leather jerkin and hat with no badge suddenly loom out of the sandstorm. He asked me if I was waiting for anything so I said, 'Yes, Montgomery'. 'Oh, I am Montgomery,' was the reply. I nearly disappeared through the ground with fright, knowing how eccentrically 'Monty' dressed. All the same I thought it couldn't be him, so picked up courage and said, 'As a matter of fact, it's *General* Montgomery I'm waiting for.' 'Oh, I see, I'm Captain Montgomery in charge of the transporters that are turning up.' My relief! Monty arrived shortly after and he spent a few minutes talking to squadron leaders and members of RHQ. This was Frank's first official appearance as second in command and he played up to it well. Immaculately dressed with field glasses over his shoulder and tight-fitting leather gloves, Monty was introduced to him; Frank saluted then started to take off his gloves which had to be done finger by finger. Monty waited patiently with his hand out till Frank had got his glove off and then shook hands!

On 8 January the tanks loaded onto transporters and proceeded to Wadi Tamet Airfield along the main road via Sirte, one night having been spent on the way. The New Zealand Division concentrated in this area before the final push to Tripoli. On the 11th I was sent off to locate the Echelons which were known to be about twenty miles to the south. I had great difficulty in finding them, many times following a mirage, which I thought was them. I saw several foxes on this trip and one or two hares. The desert in the south was as flat as a pancake and I could drive the jeep at high speed. There were several emergency landing grounds being made in the area. I at last found the Echelon and got the four lorries I was to take back ready. Going back I thought I would follow the map as opposed to going on a bearing because nearer the coast there were a lot of rolling dunes which could only be crossed in places. Soon I realized I was lost and couldn't pick up any familiar landmarks. I was convinced I was miles to the west and getting nearer the enemy but I couldn't do much about it so headed due north and I knew I must hit the coast. At last I saw some white Arab houses which I at first thought were Buerat on the front line; then to my relief I saw the vehicles of Corps HQ leaguered beside the main road which was more or less where I had hoped to come out. By this time the trucks had all overheated so we stopped for a brew and arrived back after dark. I felt relieved when I got to bed in my valise.

Another day here, Johnnie and I went to visit 4th Armoured Brigade who were some distance the far side of Wadi Tamet. On the way back we suddenly saw a gazelle grazing peacefully so we went very slowly to within twenty yards of it when I thought it would notice us. Then, accelerating fast, we chased it and Johnnie had a shot at it with my pistol. He was well below it but I think we could have got nearer still before accelerating, in which case it would have been hard to miss.

CHAPTER IX

The Pursuit to Tripoli

The Regiment moved to various concentration and staging areas on 13 and 14 January, and joined up with 2nd NZ Division – C Squadron with two troops of B Squadron to 6 NZ Brigade, and A Squadron with two troops of B Squadron to 5 NZ Brigade. At first light on the 15th the Division advanced west towards the Umm er Raml area. The Regiment, preceded by the recce vehicles of the NZ Divisional Cavalry – commonly called the 'Divvy Cav' – halted on a commanding ridge just before the Bu Ngem track. From here the Divvy Cav could be seen in difficulties in the large wadi, so the Divisional Commander ordered the Regiment to concentrate and come directly under him. The remainder of that day was spent trying to get round the flank of the enemy line of A/Tk guns and a few tanks. About an hour before sundown, enemy tanks engaged A Squadron who were soon reinforced by C Squadron and after an hour's battle the enemy withdrew, having caused no serious casualties to the Regiment. But away to the right on Dor Umm er Raml five tanks of the Sherwood Rangers (7th Armoured Division) could be seen burning. That night was spent here, protected by a Maori Battalion, which, incidentally, turned out to be unnecessary, as in the morning we found that the enemy had withdrawn.

At first light the Division advanced with a Divisional Cavalry screen in front. General Freyberg himself then led the remainder of the Division. The whole way to Tripoli he always sat outside on the front of his Honey tank with a tartan rug round his legs. The other vehicles in Tactical Division HQ were two other HQ Honeys, Colonel Sutherland (commanding Divisional Cavalry) in his Honey, the General's staff car with his ADC (aide-de-camp) and Astra with myself in it. The General kept going at a steady 20 m.p.h. which left the heavy squadrons miles behind, so I had been sent up in Astra to act as Liaison Officer. Astra was a perfect tank for this sort of 'swan', as she had no turret so could go quite fast, and as the weather was fine but cold, it was perfect sitting in my fur coat on the side in the sun with a tin of exceptionally good army biscuits beside me. The first encounter that morning was a dummy minefield which stretched right across Wadi Zem Zem up which we were going. The wire was soon cleared away and on we went. A few miles short of a very wide wadi called Soffegin, we came across many tank tracks and soon overtook three Italian M13 tanks, one being towed, the others going under their own steam. The 'Divvy Cav' only had flank screens by now, so the General himself was the first to get to these tanks. He rushed up to them, thrilled, and demanded their surrender. They were delighted at being captured – especially by so great a personality as General Freyberg! For the remainder of the journey he wore a pair of goggles which one of them had given him. He made them all line up and hand over their arms officially, while he chortled with glee – he got a delightful boyish thrill our of incidents like this. The story went round the Echelon that night that 'Mr Sprot and Mr Freyberg have captured some Italian tanks together.'

Starting off again, there was an airburst above us, followed by some shelling. This halted our 'swan' rather quickly and the Regiment was brought up to engage the enemy who were in ideal positions in the broken country where the plateau started to descend into Wadi Soffegin. Our tanks had no cover at all but in spite of that they managed to knock out a tank and many guns of varying sorts. Mirlees Chassels[1] had three tanks knocked out from under him during that short time. It was during this action that Mo was in an old Grant whose gun had not the range of the enemy ones. So, as he could not fire, he occupied himself by photographing the enemy tracer shells as they approached him. One of our casualties here was Sergeant Hooper who was killed by a piece of shrapnel. He was a fine sergeant and had been my first troop sergeant. His loss was felt, not only by his friends, but by the Regiment as a first-class tank commander.

We woke up again the next morning to find the enemy had disappeared overnight so we had to chase again at full speed. We were delayed at first by the steep escarpment down to the wadi beside the old Berber fort of Sedada which was strategically placed on a plateau of rock. There were several small dummy minefields at the top with some dummy mines – old tin cans – still waiting to be buried. The

---

1 Lieutenant M.R. Chassels, Troop Leader.

General was very amused over these. When we had got down the escarpment there was a difficult journey for the two or three miles across the wadi which was covered with clumps of thorn bushes on mounds of sand. Here 7th Armoured Division were seen quite a lot as they often had to use our tracks which were in places the only ones down certain escarpments. The column stopped for the night at last light. The last three days we had been navigating off a 1/500,000 map which showed a complete blank for this part of the desert, so we never knew exactly where we were. Luckily being with Divisional HQ, who astra-fixed our position nightly, I was able to pass the information to the Regiment.

On the 18th we made for Beni Ulid, crossing the road from there to Misurata. The deep canyon which passes through this Arab village stretched across our front. All three columns, 4th Light Armoured Brigade on the left, NZ Division in the centre and 7th Armoured Division on the right had difficulty in finding a way over. No way was found that night so we spent it peacefully and most of the next day until 6th NZ Brigade with A Squadron started off through Beni Ulid for Tarhuna to clear any mines and opposition. Later in the afternoon the remainder of the Regiment followed, luckily making the hazardously steep descent and ascent before dark. All through the village and the wadi there were abandoned M13 tanks. Sergeant Birse reported some of these in his high-pitched voice: 'I see figures three Monkey figures one three tanks. I think they are abandoned because their flaps are open and there are "wogs" around them!' After a twenty-three mile march along the Tarhuna road in the moonlight we joined A Squadron in leaguer. I had just got a mass of new maps from Division and they had to get sorted and distributed that night. I nearly went mad doing it in the wind.

The general plan the next day was for the Regiment and the Divisional Artillery to blast their way through the enemy lines south of Tarhuna. Luckily the enemy had again pulled out so we did a peace march to a spot short of Tarhuna where the General decided to wait for reports about the tracks through the hills. If we used the main Tarhuna–Tripoli road, it would mean waiting for 7th Armoured Division to go down it first. The country here was very sandy with a lot of little hillocks covered in asphodel and other vegetation. In order to get the wheeled vehicles across this hummocky ground the tanks flattened out a route, otherwise they bellied on these small mounds. The Staffordshire Yeomanry captured Tarhuna on this day and while Colonel Jim Eadie was having the keys of the town ceremoniously handed over to him, an anti-tank gun opened up from a window and everyone rather unceremoniously made a dive for their tanks and forgot about any keys!

That evening I heard General Freyberg trying to speak to General Oliver Leese, XXX Corps Commander, on the air. He was being very secure, or so he thought, and went into a long-winded sentence which started off: 'Hullo, Hullo, this is Bernard of the Kiwis. I want to speak to Oliver – you know, the Corps Commander – etc. etc.', then to finish up: 'Over and Out!' They never heard a word evidently as they asked for it all again. He had taken his hat off to speak, so pushing the headphones from his bald head, he looked round at everyone grinning and said with a chuckle 'They never heard me!'

Overnight the Divvy Cav reported a good route to the coastal plain via Tazzoli, then through the hills. It was very nippy when we woke for there had been a touch of frost that morning. I set off with Divisional HQ which led and we stopped in Tazzoli for breakfast. I thought this village with its trees, gardens and European houses quite the most beautiful place I had seen, having been in the desert so long. The Italian inhabitants were thrilled to see us and came running out cheering, including several who had been wounded by our shelling. We had a marvellous meal, produced by them, of brown bread, eggs and other delicacies. We conversed with them in a mixture of Latin and Arabic. The Regiment behind were not so lucky as they had not time so it was a case of 'One out – owner's risk'. Soon Peter B got the following message from Tim: 'Charlie Mike, your CM Two has all out. All CM to remain inside'. Poor 'Brenda',[1] who was CM 2, took some time to live that one down.

The following conversation was heard as the Regiment was crossing the open country before Tazzoli: Peter B, 'CM permission to speak to UN over.'

'CM, OK, out.'

---

1 Lieutenant H. Marshall – 'Brenda' was his nickname.

'CM to UN (Peter Paget) Charlie, Charlie on your right. over.'

'UN to CM, say again, over.'

'CM to UN Charlie, Charlie on your right, over.'

'UN to CM, say again all before "right", over.'

Then slowly and sarcastically, 'CM to UN. There *was* a fox to your right, but it has disappeared now, *out*'. Poor Peter Paj, the sight of a fox would have made his day.

Tazzoli is on the main Tarhuna–Garian road which we went along for a few miles through the most lovely hill country very like Palestine. Then, turning off, we went through a pass and emerged on the plain below to see many fires going on in Tripoli in the distance. As soon as we came out on the plain, we were Stuka-ed and Sergeant Smith in the Echelon was very badly wounded. There was a report of thirty enemy tanks on our left so the Regiment took up very well-concealed positions in the wadi, waiting for these tanks which did not materialize, and so we eventually spent the night there.

The next morning the Regiment moved over to the left, crossed the main Garian–Tripoli road in the broken country, about which several enemy tanks had been seen the previous day. Soon these same tanks were seen again and engaged. A battle then ensued for the remainder of the day. Both sides had good broken country to work in and neither suffered very serious casualties. Some local Bedouins who were encamped here took a great interest in the battle, one old man sitting beside Duggie's tank watching him and the tanks he was firing at and clapping at each shot. David Callander had his first tank brewed up here and poor Malton, his excellent servant, who was lapgunner, was killed. While crossing the road in the morning Colonel Tim asked me suddenly for our exact position. I noticed a kilometre stone a few yards away with Tripoli on it, so I snapped the reply out and hoped he would be impressed. Far from it, he merely looked at his map, and said 'Umm, don't think so, work it out.' As usual he was correct and I discovered that the '13' was an '18' which had got damaged. One always had to have the correct answer with him!

Tim, Frank and I were the three RHQ tanks – Ru must have stayed behind with the rear link – and Frank and I had been following around, when Tim suddenly got fed up with us and gave us a tremendous rocket for 'following me about like a flock of sheep'. We both turned about and were thankful to get back and have a few minutes peace and quiet. I then recced the route back to our leaguer area near a certain wind-pump. The country was so rough, I couldn't go on a bearing but luckily found a wadi that ran there. When I led the Regiment in that night in the dark, everyone was terribly impressed, thinking I had read my map in the pitch dark!

During the night 5th NZ Brigade sent patrols into Azizia to see if it was clear. If it had been we would have advanced to Tripoli during the night. However, they found it held by eight tanks and some guns, so we waited till the following morning, when the road was clear and the Division started off for the final march to Tripoli. There was an anti-tank ditch just south of Suani Ben Adem, which had a wooden bridge over it. The General was very concerned lest the tanks might break it down and he would not be able to enter Tripoli triumphantly, so we had to wait until he was across. At the crossroads at Suani, there was a mass of traffic and people conferring, arguing and gossiping. Some fully-armed Carabinieri, Italian Police, appeared out of a house much to everyone's concern, but turned out to be very helpful and organized the traffic block. Little boys were running round shouting '*Awrangis – backshish*!' The whole scene was amazing. We were told to fork left to a dispersal area which was a disappointment as it meant we would not go to Tripoli with the remainder of the Division who entered unopposed. We got hidden amongst the eucalyptus hedges and had a good brew and a wash.

In the middle of their brew, B Squadron was told to go straight off to Bianchi, an Italian colony, where General Freyberg, with one of his Brigadiers, had just been ambushed in his staff car. Just as a disgruntled B Squadron were setting off, the message was cancelled as the General had managed to crawl back along a ditch.

The arrival at Tripoli on 23 January 1943 was the end of a very big chapter in the Desert War. It fell exactly three months after the Alamein offensive started, and the Regiment covered one thousand five hundred miles, always chasing the enemy except for two short halts in the Agedabia area and at Nofilia.

CHAPTER X

Tripoli

O n arrival at our dispersal area outside Suani, we expected to move at any moment and were for the most part on three hours' notice. We eventually remained there for over seven months.

The regimental leaguer at this time of year was very pleasant with many trees. There was quite an English-looking farmyard, where Peters B and Paj used to go during 'stand-to' just to smell 'cow' in the byre! There were many violent storms during February and March and we got really wet sometimes. Then some of us would be allowed to go to an empty police post about half a mile away to light fires and dry ourselves out.

Shortly after arriving at Suani, there were two ceremonial parades. The first was a Thanksgiving Service held in the Cathedral Square in Tripoli on 31 January. David commanded the Regimental Detachment and came back with very sore feet as he had borrowed a pair of my shoes which were too small. Then on 4 February 200 men and 15 officers paraded at Castel Benito aerodrome, a short distance outside Tripoli, for a ceremonial inspection and march past with the NZ Division for the Army Commander. When the row of cars arrived it turned out that not only was Monty there but Winston Churchill and General Alan Brooke (CIGS) who had flown out especially to thank Eighth Army for capturing Tripoli and the NZ Division's part in it. While driving round the tanks Churchill was heard to remark when passing the Regiment: 'They've had a long war.' He then made a stirring speech to 'men of the New Zealand Division, the Royal Scots Greys and other attached troops'.

I unfortunately couldn't attend this as I had an ingrowing carbuncle in my arm and had to go to the Mobile Hospital in Tripoli to have it cut. It was a very uncomfortable place and the food was not up to hospital standard but I suppose, considering we had only been in Tripoli for a few weeks, it was excusable. We were still expecting to move on to Tunisia and I eventually managed to pull strings to prevent them carting me off to the Delta – what a fool I was! There was a Free-Frenchman in my ward who had lost a hand, an eye and an ear while listening to an Italian hand grenade ticking! He was very delirious and would keep on undoing his stump bandage on his wrist and the other officer and I had to rush across to stop him.

We gradually realized that we might be in Tripoli some time so started to make ourselves as comfortable as we could. Ru and I pitched an old and torn tent in amongst the most lovely wild flowers opposite the Orderly Room truck. We shared this tent till we left for Italy. The officers then started to build what became known as 'Lycett's Folly'. This was an amazing structure of corrugated iron, 44-gallon drums and wood which Michael[1] designed into an excellent Mess; it was freezing cold in winter and unbearably hot in summer but served its purpose. Cpl Walker and 'six-inch niles' Jackson did most of the work while we were more trouble than we were worth.

Poor Michael had a terrible experience one morning. He had his private Miles-Neilson (earth closet, designed by Basil Miles, our MO and Neilson, the sanitary orderly) into which, after he had finished, he used to drop a match and burn the paper for hygienic reasons. His servant also used to pour in a little petrol and light it for the same reason. This day, his servant must have run out of matches for when Michael bent down with his match, there was a 'woomph' and he lost his moustache, eyebrows, eyelashes and most of his hair, and was some time in hospital.

On 25 February the Regiment started the first of many duties undertaken in Tripoli. This was mine-watching and dock guards. Other duties that were added later on included Main Guards on HQ Tripbase, running of the Dock Smoke Screen, provision of NCOs to organize dock labour, a mobile strike force and police duties to help CMPs in clearing native cafés and brothels. The Regiment carried out all these duties really well and received praise from all quarters. Our turnout in Tripoli became a by-word in Eighth Army, and 1st Armoured Division were none too pleased when General Briggs published in Divisional orders that he expected his Division to follow the excellent example set by the Greys as regards turnout and discipline in Tripoli.

---

1 Captain M.H.L. Lycett, Squadron 2i/c.

These duties in Tripoli were carried out by one squadron per week. After Squadron HQ was bombed out of a building near the harbour it moved to a small mimosa wood known as the 'Bivvy Area' which was about three or four miles out. Then the troops on duty with two officers made their official HQ in the castle – and an unofficial one at the Del Mehari Hotel! I used to go in with A Squadron and it was great fun. We had to go round guards and mine-watching posts three times a day which took some time. Some were easily accessible round the harbour while one was on a wrecked ship in the centre. This could only be reached by boat. One day Duggie came out with 'Brenda' and me. 'Brenda', who had no idea of boats, attempted to get out onto the rope ladder from the ship, stood on the side of the dinghy and, to make things worse, hung onto the mast with a result that the boat capsized and we all had a swim. Luckily the NCO in charge of this post was none other that Cpl 'Piggy' Swain who couldn't have been more helpful producing dry clothes and hot drinks.

Another post was away out in the country at the end of the race-course. To get there one went along the motor race track and Tony Cayzer and I used to have great races in our 15 cwt trucks round it. Our evenings were usually spent in the Del Mehari which must have been a luxurious but rather immoral hotel before. It was sumptuously furnished and the bedrooms were in pairs with a bathroom between – the bath made to sit in with a step-up halfway. The dining room was a lovely place under the road and jutting right out into the harbour. We had some good parties there. I wonder if they have a new cello yet, to replace the one broken by Hugh!

Tripoli was a most pleasant town. There was the old original Arab quarter where there was a fascinating souk not unlike the Muski in Cairo. A lot of people went and bought things on first arriving at Suani. I unfortunately never managed to get there in the early days and soon it was put out of bounds on account of typhoid. The Italian quarter along the harbour was attractively laid out with gardens, palms etc., and all the main streets were lined with oleander trees about twelve feet high covered in red, pink or white flowers. There was another small Arab quarter behind the brewery where I spent many a fascinating hour watching Arabs weaving attractive silks by hand. They were of all colours and designs and I always meant to buy some lengths. In the same street was a baker and whenever I felt hungry, I would go to him, choose my loaf in the oven and eat it while it was piping hot.

Every Wednesday, organized trips were sent into Tripoli which soon gave its name to that day. When Sgt Porter, the control operator, netted in the Regiment for many months to come, he always used, as a netting call: 'Sunday, Monday, Tuesday, Tripoli Day, Thursday, etc.'

While I was in the 'Bivvy Area' one night, we saw the most spectacular sight – a heavy air raid on the docks. You could see the planes diving in and the A/A presented a solid carpet of red and yellow tracer across the sky. An ammunition ship was hit and this added to the fireworks especially when it finally blew up and scattered metal all over the promenade. Amidst all this excitement, we heard that Bob Novotny had broken a leg in a lorry accident. He was a Czech officer, who joined us at Khatatba and served us loyally the whole time. He spoke very good English but would at times come out with very funny expressions. He was an ardent Grey and we allowed him to wear the Eagle. We have not seen him since as he went back to the Czech forces when he recovered. What was their gain was our loss.

During March I had to lay out a range in the sand dunes at the back of the camp, and then drag enormous derelict lorries onto it as targets. Duggie and I spent a day doing this and successfully managed to bog down two tanks on the sand dunes with their tracks off. Before firing I used to go and visit the Mukhtar of the small Arab village in the palm trees at the back to warn them that we were going to fire. I was always given some refreshments in the form of coffee and delicious melons – those visits were most enjoyable. The local Arabs were very co-operative and it was very sad when two Arab children got killed when an unexploded shell they were playing with went off. These palm trees at the back were in little clusters and there was one beside Seymour's tank. One day he couldn't be found, and when he appeared and was asked where he had been, he replied, 'I've been having a wash in the spinny!' – a palm spinny made us laugh!

The weather that spring was exceedingly cold and we didn't change into KD (Khaki drill, our light summer uniform) until 7 April when we wore the new issue of bush shirts. The weather then became hotter and hotter and it seemed that there was a continual Khamsin all summer. Lycett's Folly registered 120° and all Johnnie's thermometers in the RAP broke. We heard later that Azizia, ten miles distant, was the hottest place in North Africa that summer. On 23 June, there were very heavy freak thunderstorms – unheard of at that time of year.

About thirty miles from the coast lies the large range of hills which we came through on 21 January. There are many delightful villages in these hills, the nearest one being Garian. Ted Rob[1] and I decided to go there one day to explore. It was a lovely journey – you climb up a lot of hairpin bends to the top of the hills, then go up and down valleys very like the Nablus-Jerusalem road. Garian itself is a tidy little town, predominantly Italian and well laid out. The native Garianites are troglodytic but we didn't visit any of their homes. We visited the large tobacco factory and were given some cigarettes – like very bad Turkish – and tobacco. We had tea in the small hotel which is one of a string run by the Del Mehari firm. I wanted sometime to go right on to Gefren, Nalut and Gadames, where there is good road the whole way and very good tourist hotels. However, I never managed it. Later we would send the Mess Sergeant to Garian where he used to buy two thousand eggs at a time.

When the hot weather began, we went into Tripoli nearly every day to bathe. There was a very good officers' bathing beach down past the Field Bakery – who, incidentally, suddenly blossomed forth with thistles on their vehicles and, to make things worse, beat us at football! Here we would spend three or four hours nearly every afternoon and evening bathing or sitting under the awning shouting for Mario to bring ices. There was a rock some way out which we used to swim out to and watch the natives fishing.

June saw two more ceremonial parades. The King's Birthday was celebrated on the 2nd and the Regiment provided two parties: a guard of honour under Alwyne[2] for General Horrocks, who took the salute; and a contingent of 130 under Peter B who followed the Navy in the march past. I was on duty at the Castle at the time and had a first-class view of it all.

After this parade we practised and beezed ourselves up madly for an inspection by 'General Lyon', which started many rumours. We were

---

1 Lieutenant E.R.W. Robinson, Troop Leader.
2 Lieutenant A.A. Compton, Troop Leader.

not surprised when, with over 500 members of the Regiment lining the
Azizia road along with 1st Armoured Division, the King appeared in
the first car. He stopped and spoke to Tim who then called for three
cheers. This happened all down the line. I'm told that HM had frightful
'gyppy tummy' and had difficulty in controlling himself.

Waterloo Day was celebrated by a whole holiday and a swimming
gala in the Jan Smuts pool.

At about this time the King's Dragoon Guards (KDG) arrived in the
area and took up residence in the blue police post beside us where they
were very well off. We all wished we had moved in there as it was so
near and would have been dry in winter and cool in summer. The Bays,
9th Lancers, 10th Hussars and 12th Lancers also came into the area so
there was quite a gathering of Cavalry Regiments.

On 10 June we were relieved of all our duties in Tripoli by 1st
Battalion The Royal Sussex Regiment and we came under command
1st Armoured Division which was not to last long for on 29 June we
came under command of 56th (London) Division.

ENSA had a very good show in Tripoli with Leslie Henson, B. Lillie,
Dorothy Dixon and many other well-known actors. We heard they were
very bored in the evenings so we arranged to give them a party. Peter
B laid it on and formed a marvellous jungle dining room in a mimosa
wood near the Bivvy Area. Palm fronds were interlaced to make the
walls and carpets spread over the sand. The food and drink might have
come from the Savoy. Everyone was in good form and after dinner we
got our guests to sing and play the piano etc. It was an excellent party
and well written up in papers at home. Some of the things B. Lillie (or
'The Lady Peel' as Frank called her) said, cannot be repeated, even here!

On 10 July Ru went to Cairo for a week's leave and I became
Adjutant for the first time while he was away. We moved that day to
our new location near Tagiura and as soon as we arrived we received
a message to the effect that the Regiment would be fully equipped
within the following two days and then sail for Sicily. A flap and a
squadron leaders' conference ensued. I was completely 'clueless' about
everything. Luckily in the middle of the conference Tony Lascelles,
GSOII AFV, Eighth Army arrived and knew nothing about us being
equipped. He said that we must have got a copy of a signal which was
sent to all units of 4th Armoured Brigade which we were supposed to

be joining. So the flap was off much to my relief. This area was a lot pleasanter being on high ground overlooking the sea and RHQ were in a small farm which was nice and cool. After about a week Lycett's Folly arrived and was re-erected.

Colonel Lugs arrived back with the Regiment having been on a lecture tour in America while convalescing. He took over command again and was immediately thrown into all the complications for the arrangements for our assault on Italy with 56th Division: waterproofing, and dryshod and wetshod training. Tanks were coming and going continually: one moment we were up to strength, the next moment we were handing them over to someone else.

As our days at Tripoli were drawing to a close, General Horrocks, X Corps Commander, under whose command the 56th Division was, paid the Regiment a visit and congratulated us on the duties, turnout and spirit of the Regiment, during the last seven months. We laid on a very smart main guard which he said was the best he had ever seen in the Middle East.

The latest secret weapon was the 17-pdr anti-tank gun with an exceedingly long barrel. Its code name was Pheasant – they certainly looked like a cock pheasant feeding, their long barrels representing the tail. I went to a demonstration by these guns firing at a pillbox. The first time it fired, the blast was so great that several people's hats were blown off. It certainly turned out to be a good weapon.

As August went on, the waterproofing and planning got more advanced. Ru was continually going to 'Mayfair', a closely-guarded block in Tripoli which was Planning HQ of 56th Division, and returning with amendments. While I was Adjutant, Tim and I had arrived in the office one morning to find a Top Secret operation order for 'Bigot Buttress' lying open on the desk. Sgt Lacey, the Orderly Room Sergeant, had opened it and consequently got a hell of a rocket. This operation was to have taken place on the north side of the toe of Italy at a place called Goia, but was later substituted by 'Bigot Avalanche', which was the eventual operation at Salerno.

We all started to take malarial precautions including that famous pill Mepachrine – 'Oaks, have you taken your Mepachrine?' was a notice which amused us later in Italy calling on 46th Division (sign – an oak tree) to take these horrible little yellow pills. They certainly immunized one from this disease and mepachrine parades were strictly enforced. Even when we returned to the UK, NCOs were still sub-consciously shouting 'Fall in for Mepachrine!' The first time we took these it affected many people very badly, and Colonel Lugs had to make a hurried exit from a dinner party given by Brigadier Julian Gascoigne at the 201st Guards Brigade.

On 14 August we moved nearer Tripoli where it would be easier to take vehicles to the docks to load up. We had a nice spot next to the Cheshire Regiment and centred round a well-to-do Italian colony. The owner was very grand and I think probably a fifth columnist as he refused to go away when Johnnie was lecturing on anti-malarial precautions. We took over the front room of his house and a small bedroom for the Colonel. He, Frank, Tim, Peter Has and Ru messed in the large room and the other HQ officers messed in a bit of Lycett's Folly which had moved yet again. It was here that Tony Cayzer got infantile paralysis, from which he never recovered sufficiently to rejoin.

I had a very amusing outing one day. We had to draw some wireless sets from the Free French Brigade who were at Sabratha, some forty miles west of Tripoli, so I set off with Tpr Jennings, who was a wireless expert but knew nothing about engines, in Peter Has's staff car. We arrived in time for lunch which I had at FF Brigade HQ – an excellent lunch in a deliciously cool marquee. I then picked up a guide and went careering off over tracks till we came to one of the Regiments. I started at RHQ where I was made to drink gin, while a very nice Adjutant arranged things. I then went to each Squadron in turn where I was made to drink more gin at each, luckily remembering to collect the wirelesses! I started off feeling very lightheaded and wishing Jennings could drive. As we were fairly early I stopped at Sabratha and went round the Roman ruins which were magnificent. I felt a bit more sure of myself after this and started off with a flourish when 'pop, pop' then silence and the car stopped. I wasn't very good on engines and Jennings knew nothing so I tinkered about with no success. Luckily a very co-operative RAF Sergeant passed in a lorry and I asked him to tow me into Tripoli. We started off, and I thought I would put it into gear and see if it would start. It did and it went like a bird. We blew our horn but couldn't get the RAF lorry to stop for miles. Eventually it did and we got home safely with our cargo.

The last few days were very hectic. I had to pack everything early as Astra had to be loaded on the ship. Charlie Radclyffe stayed on the RHQ ship to get things organized which, as you will see later, he did to no mean tune. I let him keep Smith 25, my driver, with him to look after him and my own kit on the tank. Charlie lost one of his drivers on the way and when we found him he told us that he had gone to sleep on the tank and had fallen off into the ditch; luckily he wasn't hurt.

After General Dick McCreery, who had taken over X Corps when General Horrocks had been wounded in an air raid, had lunch in the Mess on 2 September, we started off for the staging area on the race-course. The next day, the fourth anniversary of the start of the War, we left for the ships after a short prayer service, this day being a national day of prayer. I felt we were starting out on a great decisive voyage and I think it turned out to be so.

CHAPTER XI

Life in the Desert

This completes the Regiment's stay in Africa. Before embarking on the invasion of Europe both at Salerno and later in Normandy, it is worth giving an account of life in the desert and its flora, fauna, geology, and other characteristics.

The desert, as presented to most people in Beau Geste films and books, consists of endless rolling yellow sand dunes and tiny oases of a few palms and a small pool of water. This may be so in the heart of the Sahara, but not in the case of the Western Desert. Along the Alamein Line the country was hilly and gravelly and there were patches of soft sand with a few thorn bushes in them called 'ghots' – these were the bane of our existence when we got in one at night in a truck and had to dig it out. As you got nearer the great Qatara Depression there were many smaller depressions or 'Deirs' which had precipitous sides, about fifty feet or more in height, with an occasional way down. The bottom was flat and had the usual 'ghots' in them and no outlet for water, as what little rain there was soon drained or evaporated away. I have already remarked on the lovely views and sunsets that one was always seeing, especially with some of the larger features in the background. The coastal strip was different. There was an escarpment running more or less parallel to the coast about two miles or more distant from it. Between that and the sea there were flat salt pans – very dangerous to vehicles in winter – then for the last two or three hundred yards up to the sea were pure white sand dunes. Along these dunes was a considerable variety of vegetation – not thick as at home but in patches. In the winter this area along the North African coast is covered in a flower not unlike the mustard plant. There were both yellow and mauve varieties and the sight of this coloured sheet was remarkable to look at, but more remarkable to smell. After travelling fifty miles along the coast road through them, one got almost sick of them.

Further south away from the coast, flowers were few and far between and consisted almost entirely of these stubby thorn bushes. Occasionally you would find a few green shoots in some cranny in the rocks.

The Jebel Akdar – the large range of hills between Tobruk and Benghazi – cannot be classified as desert, as they are as green as any bit of Europe and have a variety of flora and fauna, unlike the desert proper. Jebel Akdar means 'the green hills'.

There were a few animals, birds, insects and reptiles that one always saw anywhere in the desert and they included snails, small lizards and beetles; I've not mentioned flies as they are obvious to anyone. These white snails covered every bush and I believe many escaped prisoners lived on them. Lizards were found in rocky places and used to scamper from stone to stone. Nice little creatures they were and many were made into pets. If you picked them up by their tails, the tail would come away and the lizard would fall and run away, its tail growing again. I only saw one large one – an iguana – and that was in Deir Ragil. It was about two feet long and looked very unpleasant.

Snakes and scorpions frequented some parts of the desert. The worst part we were in was near Charing Cross in June 1942 where there were any amount. I luckily never got stung by a scorpion but they could be very unpleasant. At Suani Ben Adem we used to find a few large spiders like tarantulas and have great sport by putting one in a tumbler with a scorpion. A tremendous fight would ensue and the scorpion usually managed to sting the spider and win.

Larger animals that were seen were gazelles, foxes and hares. How they lived in the desert was a mystery. It is said they used to drink the dew off bushes before sunrise, but for food I don't know what they did.

Birds were not very frequent visitors. I saw a hoopoe at the southern end of the Alamein Line on Quaret Humur but never saw another. A covey of chikor was put up on 'Lady Goballa' but again I never saw any more except by the coast. At Nofilia, which was only about five miles from the sea, there were a lot of bustards – a member of the turkey family. They looked enormous birds and used to flap away very slowly. Rupert Milburn found a waterhole near Agedabia out of which flew an endless stream of pigeons which presumably were rock doves.

An extraordinary thing happened when we were on the Alamein Line in August 1942. A plague of mosquitoes infested the whole area and several people went down with malaria. They are not supposed to be able to live more than a mile from water yet we were forty miles from the coast and twenty to thirty miles from Moghra Oasis. I never heard the 'school solution' to this. They may have been blown from somewhere in a gale or the Germans may have dropped them from a plane as bacteriological warfare.

I have left flies to the end as, although they existed in their trillions they were the only insect I was not pleased to see. It is impossible to give a description of these horrible things which anyone would not say was exaggeration. The food you ate was always black with them as soon as you took it out of the ration box. The more you killed, the more they seemed to multiply. In one cup of tea I had, seventy-two flies were drowned. This was in two shifts of thirty-six, which number covered the surface! Trying to have a rest in the daytime was out of the question unless you covered yourself with a blanket or something; then it was too hot. No flyproof muslin or netting was any good as it merely let them in and then they couldn't or wouldn't get out. Why there weren't more cases of madness caused by these things I don't know – I presume there must have been some cases!

Routine in the desert was always the same. Reveille an hour before sunrise, and then stand-to half an hour before till half an hour after sunrise. Even in midsummer this used to be perishingly cold and we would cluster round the exhausts in our fur coats and let the hot air blow over us. We would then brew up for breakfast – usually porridge, bacon, bread and marmalade and a mug of tea – and wash and shave in a pint or two of water, which at Alamein was not seriously rationed, although later it was. At Nofilia, all the wells were bad and we were on a strict ration of half a gallon a day and I remember shaving in the water from a tin of potatoes. The rest of the day would be spent on maintenance, patrols, range-firing or whatever the Regiment happened to be doing. Another 'brew' would be put on at midday but to eat I only had a slice of bread and cheese and tinned fruit which was sometimes in liberal supply. Another brew in the evening about five or six, which would consist of bully stew or fritter, or M and V (meat and vegetables). Everything then would be packed up for evening stand-to, half an hour before till half an hour after sunset. After this people would gather and gossip, usually over a bar of chocolate, biscuits and some whisky (that horrible Canadian Club) in a mug. Naturally this routine was only when we were static. Sometimes one went without a hot drink or meal for days on end and with two or three days' growth of beard. Cooking was always done by each vehicle itself and the chief cook of each crew used to make some marvellous inventions and concoctions. Our rations while at Alamein were extremely good and they were supplemented by grapes, mangoes and figs brought up from Alex by anyone going there.

We used to take a great pride in the cleanliness of our tanks. This used to be Colonel Lugs's pet thing and he would organize troop competitions for the cleanest tanks. He received two letters, one from the Divisional Commander and one from the Base Workshops, congratulating him on the cleanliness of the Regiment's tanks, especially the engines.

From the forward troops on the Alamein Line stretching back about ten miles was a continuous mass of vehicles and, except when in a depression, you could never get out of sight of a vehicle of sorts – very useful if you broke down. Running amongst these was a maze of minefields, all marked with wires and gaps. There were not many places you could go to by reading a map or on a bearing as you were bound to strike one of these. You had to have the gaps marked on your map as there were many tracks marked with certain signs – C, inverted T, S, Boomerang etc. The minefields and gaps all had names which would be in blocks – Nuts and May; January and February; Cochran, June and Inverclyde, and other such combinations.

During the time I spent in the desert I found it had a great attraction and I think that, being so devoid of animals and vegetation, when you did come across something, you appreciated it all the more.

PART II — ITALY

CHAPTER XII

The Assault on Salerno

On 3 September 1943, after a long march from the Tripoli racecourse to the docks, we all went aboard our various LSTs[1] and LCTs.[2] Luckily, being RIO, I was with RHQ on an LST where Charlie Radclyffe had been for the past few days preparing things for us. LSTs only have accommodation for twelve officers but on this one there were somewhere in the region of fifty. So we were indeed lucky that Charlie had fixed us up to share cabins with the ship's officers. Colonel Lugs (as OC Ship) was in the Captain's cabin; Ru was in his sitting room; Charlie was with the First Officer; Peter Downie was with the engineer officer; Padre Mac was with the Second Officer and myself with the Navigator. All the other officers with the exception of the twelve most senior ones were stuck down in the hold. Our ship was number 401 and that afternoon we moved out of the harbour and lay at anchor overnight, sailing on the 4th. On 5 September we were lying off Biserta and after a church service on board, the front of the craft was lowered and everyone bathed off it in perfect weather although the previous day had been rough. We remained there till the 7th and had one air raid with no damage, and later that day they tried to fix pontoons to the side of the RHQ ship. These were long, flat floats which are run ashore so that vehicles could drive in dry-shod over them. They were about thirty or forty yards long and very cumbersome; they only managed to fix one on.

After sailing on the 7th the Colonel assembled all troops and gave out the plan for the invasion of Italy by Fifth US Army in Salerno Bay. We realized we couldn't be far off Italy now, although we kept up our normal routine of PT and other games to amuse and exercise ourselves. There was a very comfortable wardroom but, owing to the great number of officers, it was always crowded and meals had to be served in three shifts.

1 Landing Ship Tank.
2 Landing Craft Tank.

On the evening of 8 September, excitement ran high as the Commodore's ship was flying a signal and our crew couldn't read it, or they thought they couldn't, because it seemed to say 'Italy has surrendered'. But having checked it back, it was correct.

It was considered a bad thing to give this out the day before we were to invade the country because all felt that the landing would be unopposed and it would be a matter of 'quickest the best to the Brenner'. As we were to see the next day, it was completely the opposite, the Germans being very relieved to get rid of their Italian 'Allies' and fighting all the harder.

Whatever people thought about it, everyone celebrated as much as possible at such a time. I've never seen so much bukshee rum that seemed to turn up from nowhere. In spite of the celebrations, we all got to bed early, or at least to lie down, as we were not allowed to undress this last night. At about 4 a.m. on the 9th the sirens blew the alarm which was for stand-to as we were approaching the coast. I got up and saw the ship's navigator in the next bunk was still asleep and tried to wake him, but he was suffering from the celebration and didn't come to till some time after the ship had ground ashore!

Salerno Bay was an amazing sight, thick with shipping of all shapes and sizes, some being off-loaded on the shore, some transferring their loads to a smaller craft; a lot of movement of vehicles and men on the beach; the odd 'brew-up' on both the shore and the sea; guns firing out to sea and big ships returning the fire; rocket ships making the most infernal din as they set off their rockets. During all this we had to cruise about waiting our turn to come ashore, which we did not do till four o'clock in the afternoon.

As usual, in a rather grim period, there are always the funny moments. All the officers, mostly the older ones, were on the bridge watching how things were going, when an anti-tank gun opened up on us and sent AP shot one after the other alternately each side of us. As soon as one landed on the starboard side everybody ran to the port side; then one landed on the port side and everyone came running back; and so it went on. A German OP might have been watching it through glasses and doing it for fun, for indeed it was comical. These elderly officers were mostly members of AMGOT – Allied Military Government Occupied Territories – but more commonly known as Ancient Military Gentlemen On Tour!

The Salerno Landing. Disembarking from Landing Ships (Tank): Tanks of B Squadron and a Reconnaissance Troop carrier can be seen

Later in the day Charlie and I were looking out of the wardroom porthole when Charlie, trying not to get excited, suddenly remarked, 'I say old boy, do you see what I see? Isn't it the periscope of a submarine?' I must say it did look like one if you hadn't seen the ship towing this object which was a mine-cutting vane.

It was here that we first saw DUKWs in action. They are amphibious jeeps and they would go about in droves of ten or so with a launch in charge of them, looking like a mother duck with her ducklings fussing round her.

We eventually got a dry-shod landing after several attempts to get the ship in. The Captain's golden labrador was very pleased to see land again but very annoyed when he found he wasn't allowed off. Frank and John Warrender landed earlier in order to recce an area for us so they directed us straight to a field only two or three hundred yards from the beaches. We pulled off the waterproofing from the tanks here and saw in the next field where A Squadron had de-waterproofed.

The country here was marvellous after Africa. There were grass fields and verges to the roads, running water, green hills, flowers and fruit everywhere. For about six miles inland, it was dead flat with dykes criss-crossing every hundred yards. Then like an amphitheatre the hills formed a semi-circle right round, making a most impressive view. I had a set of semi-oblique photos of the coast, places on which I had been able to pinpoint on the map. This made it fairly simple to see exactly where we landed which was just to the south of the River Tusciano.

The field next to ours was planted with Italian 'plum' tomatoes which we soon found out were a common crop in that area. They were just at their height so everyone soon had their ration boxes full and I don't think any were ever empty for the next month or two.

CHAPTER XIII

Fighting in the Beachhead

The three Sabre Squadrons were attached, one each, to the three Brigades of 56th Division – A Squadron with 167 Brigade (Ox & Bucks, two battalions of Royal Fusiliers), B Squadron with 201 Guards Brigade (Grenadiers, Coldstream and Scots) and C Squadron with 169 Brigade (three battalions of Queens). A & C Squadrons were with the two assault Brigades which were to assault the beaches either side of the Tusciano River, and B Squadron with 201 Brigade who were to land later in reserve. The two Brigades objectives were Montecorvino Aerodrome on the left for 169 Brigade and Battipaglia (commonly called Batty P) for 167 Brigade.

Shortly after first light, Duggie's LCT was hit and his tank received a direct hit on the turret which caused it to brew and soon the whole craft was on fire. The ship was abandoned and people had to swim for it. Luckily they were only 150 yards from the shore which they reached safely either by swimming or being picked up by small launches. Unfortunately Lieutenant W.J.S. Hutcheson, who had just joined before sailing and two other ranks were killed. Duggie was burned about the face and hands and stayed for a bit at RHQ, so Mo commanded A Squadron the first day till Frank took over.

Both Squadrons had a difficult time as their infantry were very green. The Royal Fusiliers were attacked by flame-throwing tanks – a secret weapon in those days – which somewhat demoralized them. Two of these tanks were later knocked out by A Squadron. They didn't make much headway towards Batty P but consolidated on a line about two and a half miles from the beaches. On the left 169 Brigade and C Squadron were unable to take the airfield although one troop got round it at one moment. David had another tank knocked out from under him. Massey was very unfortunate here as shortly after landing, 'Danny' Radclyffe drove his tank 'Wob Woy' into a ditch and there it remained filling up with water and all his kit in it. After several days, they eventually got it out with the aid of 'D8' tractors. B Squadron and their

Brigade had landed and were concentrated in reserve. That evening was very unpleasant as no one knew what the position exactly was. The beachhead was only two to three miles deep and 46th Division on our left had not been very successful.

The next week was also unpleasant; the enemy, seeming to get stronger, put in attacks at all weak portions of the line. Until 12 September C Squadron remained in the area of Montecorvino Airfield and the high ground to the north of Route 8 and was the least disturbed Squadron. B Squadron and 201 Brigade had been directed on Batty P and had a very unpleasant time astride the railway just to the west of the town where one troop got onto the main road and held a bridge on the outskirts. They also had much fighting round the tobacco factory there. A Squadron were still with 167 Brigade on the right and had great difficulty in keeping their infantry from withdrawing. On one occasion just as the Squadron was returning to leaguer, it was reported that the infantry and gunners were 'fleeing in confusion' and the Squadron was ordered to return to assist. When they had got back not only did they find that the infantry and gunners were not there, but the enemy were not either and never had been, as all their guns, etc. were still in position with ammunition untouched. Doubtless, their officers had seen our tanks going back to leaguer and had mistaken them for enemy which they did many a time at close range.

On 12 September the Colonel attended a conference at 56th Division HQ where it transpired that all Squadrons would come under command of the Regiment instead of being split up. Consequently that evening the Regiment assembled in a pleasant grass field, centred on a clump of trees. The Senior Chaplain at Division was Padre Brown, the Kent County Cricketer, who was always far more in the picture than most of the staff and Colonel Lugs would always ask him for the latest information or the whereabouts of certain units, knowing he would always get the answer – a most popular man and a great asset to a Divisional HQ.

It was in this new area that we were in direct line of fire from HMS *Warspite* and a monitor lying in the bay. It was a strange sound when they fired, for you would first hear the crack which was the shell going overhead, then came the report of the gun firing, then the explosion away in the hills – three different reports.

The weather was exceedingly warm and there was no rain which was lucky, as we had no shelter at night. However, Frank's head felt the cold a bit at night for when doing a stalk down a hedgerow, whilst commanding A Squadron, he had taken his beret off and dropped it. He couldn't find it and couldn't get a new one until B Echelon arrived the following week.

One day going through the beachhead in the jeep with the Colonel, I suddenly saw Peter Wyld, in the Coldstream, a great friend of mine, on the road. I yelled at him, and the Colonel jammed on the brakes in an awful state, thinking at least I had been shot. When he discovered what I was shouting about he was not pleased!

We still continued to live on tomatoes and apples, although unfortunately there were no grapes or figs in this area. One day the Colonel and I found an old man who said he had some honey in the tobacco factory at St Lucia. He was on a bicycle so we told him to lead on, and Miller, who was driving us, to follow. Miller had not driven the Colonel for long and I think was a bit nervous so tried to do everything exactly as he was told; hence the reason for following the 'Itie' down a footpath and over a rosebed before we could stop him!

From 12 September, when the Regiment came under command of 23rd Armoured Brigade, until the 17th, the Regiment was on 167 Brigade front which stretched from the River Tusciano to St Lucia. Most days there was a flap on of some sort which sent the whole of the Regiment up. One evening a report came through that the enemy had put in an attack and our infantry were making for the beaches. All Squadrons, Recce Troop and RHQ went up to the front and took up positions. There was a continual stream of infantry coming back down the road, so Tim Readman stood in the middle and when they asked him the way to the beaches he replied in his calm, unhurried way, 'Um! You're going the wrong way, the beaches are over there,' pointing at the front line. They all turned innocently around and went back.

There was a certain officer from a formation HQ who came back and said that he was going to organize the shipping on the beach to take everyone off. Unfortunately for him, he was speaking to Colonel Lugs! This same night, the Colonel and I paid a visit to a Battalion of the Hampshire Regiment who were the 'Beach Brick', responsible for administration in the beachhead. Their CO made more of an impression on us than all the other infantry battalions put together. He was quite old and a real 'Poona' Colonel. His spirit was marvellous and he instilled it into all his men who were waiting about mad keen to have a crack at the enemy. When he spoke, everything was in terms of Rupees and 'fast running coolies' (meaning a DR). Mike Hall[1] had spoken to him the day before and they were talking about a Battalion of Hampshires to whom Mike was attached at the beginning of the War. Mike asked him if he knew their CO whom he described as a 'typical Old Indian who was a bit too fond of his gin'. The old man replied with a roar of laughter: 'Why, damn it, that was me!'

Charlie Radclyffe was in charge of RHQ that night and he was walking round the tanks when he heard someone approaching.

'Halt, who goes there?' No reply and the noise continued.

'Halt, or I'll fire.' Still it came on.

'Halt or really I will fire.' Then he never heard or saw the noise again. That was a stock joke for some while.

Another day there was a flap on the American front to our right and we were told to be ready to counter-attack the enemy who were expected to try and force through to the coast thereby separating the US Corps from X Corps. The Colonel, squadron leaders and myself went on a most delightful recce over in the American sector very nearly as far as the Sele River. The country there was undulating with large fields of grass and hedges and was such a pleasant change to the flat area round Batty P. Our maps of that area were very bad and I'm afraid I got a bit lost once or twice.

A heavy infantry attack was put in early one morning and the whole Regiment went up to man the small canal running alongside the road between the Tusciano and St Lucia. RHQ was in St Lucia farm and when Denis Symington[2] was asked where we were he replied, 'We are at the name of a famous tune Tra-la-la-la-la' – singing St Lucia over the air which was probably a tune as well known to the Hun as to us – not very secure! This day, C Squadron did a sweep out in front of the position from left to right. Unfortunately Roy Howard's[3] tank was knocked out and it was not learned till later that he had died soon

---

1   Lieutenant M. Hall, Troop Leader.
2   Lieutenant D. Symington, Troop Leader.
3   Lieutenant J.R. Howard, Troop Leader.

after. Someone is supposed to have heard the Germans giving out over the air about Roy's tank being hit and he having died. This action was well described in the *Cavalry Journal* in an article on 23rd Armoured Brigade's fighting in Italy:

Ordeal and Fulfilment – The story of the 23rd Armoured Brigade

It was in a sense appropriate that, when the Allied armies split into two up the backbone of Italy, the Brigade should have been divided between them and so, by strange destiny, have continued to reflect the history of the Allied war effort. On 9th September, the Brigade, less 46th and 50th Royal Tanks, but with the Royal Scots Greys temporarily under command, landed on the beaches of the wide bay of Salerno.

The story of that sad disillusionment is well known. Of how Italy had surrendered on the evening before the landings; how the true temper of German resistance in Europe was there first felt; how the suspense mounted, and the eyes of the free and the enslaved world were hypnotised by the struggle of that small arc of treacherous Italian soil.

On the 16th September, the Brigade commanded a sector of the perimeter on the junction of the British and American corps in the beach-head. On that day, the full German counter-attack was launched to cut the beach-head in two. The Greys were held in reserve until the British line had been pushed back by five hundred precious yards and every man in the echelons stood-to in a defensive position. Then they were unleashed to counter-attack, and striking across the flanks of the enemy's penetration, by midday had restored the position. Two hundred of the German assault infantry were lying killed on the ground. The next day the enemy began to withdraw from the beach-head.

(Extract from the *Royal Armoured Corps Journal* Vol 1, No. 1, July 1946, by kind permission of the Editor.)

After the sweep, the Regiment, with the infantry, gradually pushed back to the original line. Recce Troop were ordered to find out if a certain farm was clear, so Corporal Benton set off in his carrier, standing upright in the front smoking his pipe. When he got to the farm, he got out, knocked on the door and shouted in asking if there were any Germans there. No reply, so he came back and reported it was clear – which was the case.

Our way to and from our assembly area and the front was by road to a large farm called 'Porte de Ferro', and then across country. This farm had many large paddocks where all the Shetland ponies from some big Italian circus were evacuated. There were forty or fifty and of all different colours and sizes.

During the first few weeks after the landing, there were codewords for challenges and replies. They would always be in pairs such as: 'Tennis-Racket', 'Edinburgh-Castle', and other such combinations. The sentries often used to get muddled and so did the person who was challenged and they would be said the wrong way round or the one being challenged would say his bit first and there would be frightful confusion, or else they would both burst out laughing. One night the challenge was 'California', to which someone replied 'Syrup of figs', quite subconsciously, whereas the real reply was 'Oranges'. This completely foxed the sentry.

On 17 September, Peter Has arrived with the '1st follow up'[1] which consisted of most of B Echelon, and in the evening the Regiment moved over towards Salerno to an orchard by the village of Pontecagnano-Faiano. The enemy were starting to withdraw on the whole front and we had a new role in store.

In the last nine days' fighting the Regiment lost many fine and irreplaceable officers and other ranks, killed, wounded and taken prisoner. Two troopers, who were taken prisoner, escaped back and told us that, when they were being questioned, the German officer said to them, 'We know your Squadron Leaders are Borwick, Roborough, and Stewart and your Commanding Officer is F-I-E-N-N-E-S but we don't know how to pronounce it. Is it Fee-ens or Fines?'

---

1 The first part of the administrative vehicles.

CHAPTER XIV

Left hook to Naples

We spent 18 September peacefully in the orchard at Pontecagnano -Faiano, everyone being relieved at the news that the enemy was undertaking a major withdrawal and that Eighth Army had joined up properly.

I went with Brigadier Harry Arkwright, commanding 23rd Armoured Brigade and known in the Regiment as Waahid Shufti, Arabic for 'one look' because he wore a monocle, and the Colonel on a recce in the hills behind Faiano where we had a marvellous view of the entire Bay of Salerno laid out at our feet. It was packed with shipping of all shapes and sizes and the flat country where we had been fighting for the last ten days was a mass of vehicles or dumps. It was in this area that a German OP's diary was found, describing what he saw on the morning of 9 September, when our invasion fleet had arrived off the coast. To the north there was a grand view across the valley of the River Picentino, which formed a large basin, to the village of S. Cipriano and the high hills behind. We climbed onto the roof of a small farm, which was right on the top of the hill, to see this view and the old farmer told us that the well he fetched his water from was in the hollow on the enemy side and he had to be very quick about drawing it when the Germans were not using it. Returning, we stopped at a Naval OP which was very comfortably situated on the terrace in front of the Montecorvino Monastery whose monks were continually bringing them fruit, tea, wine, and grapes. We stayed with them for a bit and watched them fire *Warspite* which was lying in the Bay. It was fascinating watching her guns fire; you would see a puff of smoke as they fired; then you could eat two or three grapes and a fig or two and be in time to watch the shell burst on some bridge or other target, many miles inland.

That evening we heard the Regiment's role for the immediate future. This was to be part of a column under 23rd Armoured Brigade which was to cross the hills west of Salerno, so forcing the enemy to abandon the pass through which the main Salerno-Naples road ran. So the next morning all the tanks loaded onto LCTs and went along the coast to the village of Maiori. Wheeled vehicles went by road which entailed a hazardous crossing of the bridge at Vietri, just beyond Salerno. There was an enemy strongpoint in the hills from which could be seen the bridge and they had great fun in machine-gunning our vehicles as they crossed. Many raids were made to liquidate this strongpoint but with no success. This bridge was well controlled by MPs; vehicles were halted just before reaching it; then one by one they were sent across as fast as possible. This was a dangerous operation as there was a right-angled corner both onto and off the bridge which was about seventy yards long. The Colonel and I got safely past in the jeep in spite of rather reckless driving by Cpl Miller. A lorry of ours having successfully negotiated the bridge went too near the side of the road which gave way and it careered down a sheer drop of some 100 feet or more. Luckily it was the only lorry without a hood, so Sgt Russell and his driver were able to jump out and hang on to a tree. The lorry remained a crumpled wreck for as long as we were in Italy.

The journey along the coast to Maiori was most delightful. The road twisted and turned alongside the hills with a sheer drop into the sea on the one side and terraced vineyards climbing the hills on the other. Every now and again there would be a small fishing hamlet nestling in a cove with nets hanging out to dry, and upturned boats. Maiori itself was a large village with a pleasant beach, and a valley running back into the hills through which the route ran over to Naples by the small twisty road we were to take.

There were no fields flat enough for the Regiment to bivouac in so the Colonel selected sufficient houses as billets. After that, he and I and the Brigadier went up to the pass at the top which was held by American Rangers. From Maiori to the top was about eight miles and the road twisted and turned up this valley past vineyards, farms and monasteries. On arrival at the top we were rewarded with another of the superb views one gets in Italy. The whole of the Neapolitan plain lay below with Vesuvius, belching smoke, standing like a sentinel in the middle and Pompeii and the other suburbs of Naples at her feet. The Island of Ischia lay out to sea shining like a jewel set in blue velvet. We were sitting on a low wall admiring this view and forgetting that a war existed when we were brought back to reality by a whistling noise getting louder and louder, nearer and nearer. We all dived behind a pile of stones when there was an almighty explosion above us and we were covered in gravel. We clambered up in the dust and discovered that a large shell had burst on the cliff about fifteen feet above us. The Colonel had been holding his telescope and a small piece of shrapnel had cut very neatly between the thumb and forefinger and then gone through the telescope much to his annoyance. The Brigadier complained that something had gone into his back by his shoulder blade. I was thanking my lucky stars that I had not been hit; I had only felt a bit of something hit my back, but someone noticed that my shirt was all blood and it turned out that I had a small wound in my back. We all bundled into our jeeps and went back at a high rate of knots. Cpl Miller was very good, shouting at everyone to get out of the way as he had two 'very seriously wounded officers on board!' We were both feeling quite alright and very amused by all this.

We were taken to the little monastery in the village which had been turned into an emergency aid station by the Americans with whom we were working. I was laid out on a bed in the main church whilst they looked at my back. Luckily it was an 'in and out' which didn't go deep and went between two ribs. They bandaged me up and I joined the Brigadier and the Colonel in a ward upstairs. We spent two days here doing nothing much, and then returned to the Regiment when my knee started to get very stiff so I went back to the hospital for them to have a look at it. They decided it was a small piece of shrapnel which had gone in without me noticing it. So I was put under and woke up later with my leg in plaster which was sticking to the wound, through which they had tried unsuccessfully to locate the piece, making it very painful. I spent a very miserable four days there. The hospital was far from comfortable and staffed by Yanks who meant well but behaved in such a completely different way to our Medical Orderlies. After I was fit to walk I went back to B Echelon in an ambulance and was very frightened going over the Vietri bridge but luck was with me again and we were not fired at.

The night I arrived back in B Echelon, the first rains came and I, who was sleeping outside, got absolutely soaked and felt as if I was lying amongst a heap of wet sheets and blankets in the laundry. As my leg was in plaster I couldn't move my bed and belongings so had to lie there till daylight in this deluging storm. That morning Peter Has tried to get some ammunition and petrol wagons out of the leaguer but they got so firmly stuck in the mud that it took well over an hour to pull them out with the Scammell recovery vehicles.

I had my plaster removed in an ADS which had taken over a farm-house in Pontecagnano. As I was limping, I asked then for a stick and they gave me a fascinating Italian shepherd's crook which belonged to the farm. This stick did me good service for the remainder of our time in Italy and I still use it at home.

While I was in hospital and back at B Echelon the officers with the Regiment had been having a marvellous time at all the local seaside resorts, like Ravello and Amalfi, where everyone was delighted to see them and produced some excellent local Caruso wine called Lachrimi Christi, some of which I had with Peter; it was certainly very good. I was very annoyed at missing this week of gaiety.

On 30 September I started off for the Regiment in a lorry taking up supplies. I was not sure which was the best way – by the main road via Cava or by the hill road from Maiori. The going was very slow owing to the amount of traffic. I passed Tony Bonham[1] who had just arrived with the 'Balance to WE'.[2] At Vietri I decided to try the main road but after a couple of miles I realized I should never get along it within a month of Sundays as there was so much traffic, so we turned round and stopped for the night on the roadside just short of Vietri. Next morning, after an excellent breakfast, for Moffat the cook was on my lorry, we started off and had a good run; the first time I had been across the Vietri bridge without the thought of being fired upon. We continued via Maiori over the top where I had been wounded and down a very steep hill with a myriad hairpin bends. Halfway down we came upon one of our tanks on its side at the edge of the road. Looking up we could see that it had hurtled down from the road above. It was poor Graham Plews's[3] tank. He was sitting on the outside when the road gave way underneath and it started to fall down the hill, but he managed to jump clear. Cpl Shepherd, his gunner, was also on the

---

1 Captain Sir A.L.T. Bonham Bart., HQ Squadron 2i/c.
2 'Balance to War Establishment' being the remainder of the transport of the regimental supply column.
3 Lieutenant G.R. Plews, Troop Leader.

outside and must have got buried by the tank for he was not found, while we were in the neighbourhood, although people dug all round. I don't think Graham ever got over this; sadly he was killed a month later.

We found 23rd Armoured Brigade HQ in the village of Angri and they directed us on to the Regiment who were by now on the outskirts of Naples. I found them in leaguer in Torre Annunziato where they had a bit of a battle and Sgt Maclauchlan had been killed.

CHAPTER XV

Capture of Naples
and advance to the Volturno

This was the first time we had been in a civilized European town since leaving Britain many years before; everyone was excited and there were rumours of British people turning up, of Fascist houses being burned down, and other such incidents.

Colonel Lugs had a huge army under him consisting of an A/Tank Battery, a Recce Squadron and a company of Texas Rangers, and there were American LOs at RHQ who were terribly excited at the idea of being in Naples on the morrow.

Frank had a touch of malaria that evening and was very depressed sitting on the pavement in his chair.

On 1 October the Regiment entered Naples like liberators. A Squadron of KDGs led to start with but we overtook them just before Naples proper, and it was exceedingly hard work making any headway through the dense cheering crowds. It was exactly like the crowds in front of Buckingham Palace on Coronation night, except here you had every balcony and window crowded and covered in anything that provided a display of colour, whether it be bedspread, flag, dishcloth or flowers. The vehicles were mobbed and everyone had bottles of wine and fruit pressed into their hands. The flowers on the tanks camouflaged them better than Duggie ever did with tobacco plants! Pamphlets were distributed of which the following is a copy (sic):

Brothers,
after thirtynine months of war, pains and grieves; after twenty years of tyranny and inhumanity, after having been the innocent victims of the most perverse gang at the Government; today, September 8th 1943, we can cry at full voice our joy, our enthusiasm for your coming.

We can't express with words our pleasure, but only we kneel ourself to the ground to thank God, who have permit us to see this day.

With you we have divided the sorrow of the war, with you we wish to divide the day of the big victory. We wish to march with you, until the last day, against the enemy N. I. We will be worth of your expectations, we will be your allied of twenty-five years ago.

Hurra the allied
Hurra the free Italy.

The Committee of antifacist ex fighters of the big war

All this less than a month after they ceased to be our official enemies.

While we were forcing our way through this mêlée, one would see the Colonel charging about with a pick-helve knocking civilians off the tanks.

We soon got a message to say we were not to go through Naples but were to keep round the east and north sides in order to safeguard our right flank which had been left exposed owing to 7th Armoured Division's slow progress on our right. There was a bit of a halt whilst a route was found and Mike dealt with some Germans holding out in a graveyard at Barra. The Colonel and I went into a room opposite where our tank was, so that we could lay our maps out in reasonable peace. We were soon joined first by Brigadier Harry Arkwright and then by General Mark Clark, Commander Fifth US Army. When we came out to start off again, the Army Commander used my tank's wheel to relieve nature against – surely an almost unique experience for a Subaltern's tank!

We spent that night in the small village of Poggiore and I had difficulty in finding the way back to Brigade Tac HQ where the Colonel had a conference. However, when we got there we were ushered into the Brigadier's caravan out of the rain, then given a whisky and soda!

It was a drenching day on 2 October and not much progress was made. The Regiment moved slowly through the outskirts of Naples past the airfield and the Rotunda and stopped at the last house as the road in front was blocked by trees, and B Squadron, who were trying to get round by the left, were held up by a blown bridge at Marianella. A Squadron and Recce Troop had a few minor engagements on the right in Casoria and Arzano. Brigade HQ had moved into a large cemetery on the hill leading up to the Rotunda and it was rather gruesome as we all sat round on gravestones or sheltered in tombs.

The entry into Naples

While the Colonel and I were there General Erskine of 7th Armoured Division arrived and said how very well the Brigade, and especially the Regiment, had done in the advance up to and through Naples.

After a wet night, the advance continued with ourselves and the KDGs leading together. A way was found round the outskirts of Naples via Miano and Marianella and thence, it was hoped, via Mariano-Di-Napoli to Qualiano, but there was another blown bridge short of Mariano and the enemy were in Mugnano, the only alternative way. An attack was laid on by B Squadron, with the aid of American infantry, to clear Mugnano and Giugliano-in-Campagnia, inevitably coded to 'Country Guy' by Colonel Lugs.

The undergrowth was very thick and due to this and well-concealed enemy positions the attack failed. Seymour, who was supporting this attack, was in one of his long-winded, insecure moods and started to explain exactly where he was going in relation to the church steeple. He was quickly hushed by Peter B.

While Ted Robinson's troop was in the area, there was much shelling and crews were not allowed out of their tanks unless permission was given by the troop leader. The following conversation on the air was heard between Ted and Sgt Dickinson, his troop sergeant, whose call-sign was 'William one Abel'. He always seemed to have this callsign and soon became known as that.

Sgt D: 'William one able, may I get out, over.'

Ted: 'William one able, umm, why? Over.'

Sgt D: 'William one able, I want to go to the lavatory, over.'

Ted: 'William one able, umm, is it urgent? Over.'

Sgt D: 'William one able, yes it is, over.'

Ted: 'William one able, well, umm, if you must, you must, over.'

Sgt D: 'William one able, I *must*, out'.

RHQ was centred round a small house on the main road and the flat rooftop made an excellent OP. From it, we had our first sight of Caserta Palace, that huge building, larger than Buckingham Palace, fifteen miles away.

On 4 October, it was learnt that the Americans had cleared 'Country Guy', so the Regiment moved forward to Qualiano – naturally coded to 'Quags' – with A Squadron supporting a squadron of KDGs. This last advance had been so quick that many demolitions, which had been prepared, were not set off. In Quags a nasty sight was seen – the bodies of a priest and some children who had been lined up and shot by retreating Germans. No wonder we found a large notice in twelve-inch lettering in the next village which read: 'Welcome to our liberators, out fucking Germany!'

Colonel Lugs was always full of ideas for code names for towns. Besides those mentioned other typical ones were 'Duggie' for Frignatoro and 'Cedric' for Cellole – Sgt Cedric Lacey's instrument in the band being the cello.

About two miles short of Villa Literno, the Regiment was stopped and told to form a firm base round a crossroads so that the American Airborne Regiment could patrol actively through Villa Literno to the Volturno River. While Alwyne was sitting in his tank on the road he suddenly saw an old German telephone line at the side of the road moving forward. He reported it as queer, he being the leading vehicle, and we never discovered what it actually was. We leaguered that night in a small farm and the outhouse we slept in had a mass of walnuts drying on ledges. As the ground was very wet, we laid our bedding on the walnuts which were surprisingly comfortable, or else we were all very sleepy and didn't feel them. The farm became known as 'Walnut Farm'.

The next day the Regiment moved forward to Villa Literno and A Squadron supported the American Bridgehead over the Regi Lagni Canal, three miles short of the river. There were many demolitions in this area which made movement difficult. On 6 October, we were informed that the Regiment would again come under command of 56th (London) Division on the right flank of X Corps, for the crossing of the Volturno. So on the 7th the Regiment moved via Albanova and Aversa to an area round a farm between the main Naples–Capua road and the village of Marcianise. Recce Troop had guides out at road junctions, and I was very annoyed with Sgt Morton who was sheltering from the pelting rain under a bridge and consequently let us take a wrong turn. Having gone a short distance I realized I was wrong so the whole column had to turn round. The area where we went to was deep in mud and it was rightly called 'Misery Farm' – its Italian name being Misere.

CHAPTER XVI

The Volturno to the Savone di Riardo

Misery Farm was our home from 7-16 October. During that time, I don't think we had one decent day; it rained most of the time and the whole area became a quagmire. The squadrons were, unfortunately, in the open, RHQ being the only lucky ones in the farm itself.

The first few days here were spent in preparing for the assault of the River Volturno in the Capua area with 167 Brigade. Seymour Pears, Alwyne Compton, Alec Lewis and Denis Symington went on patrol the first two nights with the infantry to recce possible crossing places, but owing to the steepness of the banks, none was found. Alec was always keen on a bit of excitement and asked especially to go as it was his birthday!

The Colonel, with his usual host of ideas, invented a float made of sheaves of flax which had just been harvested. He and Mr Anderton (the RSM) discovered that three sheaves tied together were sufficient to carry two men. General Erskine, GOC 7th Armoured Division came to see a demonstration and was much impressed. John Hope and Jonathan Blow, Brigade Major and Intelligence Officer 201 Guards Brigade, were made to go for a row on one of the floats. They got their bottoms a bit wet, otherwise it was highly successful. They were never used in the actual crossing but plans were afoot to make them if there was a shortage of craft.

The HQ of 56th Division was situated at the enormous palace at Caserta. It is a magnificent building centred round three large quadrangles. Divisional HQ was mostly in the beautifully laid out gardens and only used a bit of the building as a mess. There was a broad vista running from the centre of the building through gardens, then up the hill in the distance. Down this hill was a series of fountains or cascades and it was a fine sight standing by the palace looking up the vista and seeing the water tumbling down the waterfalls from one fountain to the other. The little 'Fox Cub' command planes could land on the garden paths and were parked under the trees.

The nearest town was Santa Maria where we often went to, as 169 Brigade HQ was on the racecourse there. The shops seemed to be full of everything, especially cakes and sweets. They made delicious nut toffee and most tanks had a large tin ammunition box full for the remainder of our days in Italy.

On 12 October, the main attack across the river started. A Squadron's role was to cross the river if possible with 167 Brigade whilst C Squadron took up positions where they could give covering fire. RHQ moved up to a farm near the small village of S. Tamarro. A Squadron and RHQ had been waterproofed for this operation. Astra, my Stuart tank, had been done in a special way which was unsuccessful, as the exhaust fumes came back into the driving compartment, and Smith was overcome by them, so we had to rip off the waterproofing before proceeding.

No news was received as to how the attack was going till just before midnight when 9 RF Battalion HQ returned to our farm to say that the attack was unsuccessful and had been called off. So we all turned about and went back to Misery Farm. We heard afterwards that the Commanding Officer of another Battalion had been put under close arrest by his Intelligence Officer (a Subaltern) for being drunk just before H-Hour. Hugh, needless to say, wrote one of his appropriate 'Odd Odes' about this.

Two days later, another assault across the river by daylight was ordered as it was thought that the enemy had pulled out. However, as is usual on these occasions, enemy fire was heavier than normal, so it was cancelled. That evening the Colonel was informed of the plan by which 56th Division would cross by the American bridge which spanned the river where it entered the plain having cut its way through the hills. B Squadron were to be attached to 201 Guards Brigade and C Squadron to 2/6 Queens for the advance after crossing the river. The information about the bridge was that it was Class 30, so A Squadron were ordered to de-waterproof; no sooner had they done this than a LO arrived to say that the bridge was Class 9; all waterproofing had to go back on again till that evening when another message was received to say it was Class 30 after all, so off it all came again!

On the 15th C Squadron crossed the river in the afternoon and leaguered with their infantry at a farm called Trilisco. The rest of the

Regiment remained at Misery Farm and during the day the Colonel and I went up the hill overlooking the bridge with several other officers from the Division. It was quite a long climb but one had a marvellous view from the top looking west across the Plain of Naples with the Volturno winding its way through, and east into the mass of the Appennines. Straight opposite was a small hill with a building, probably a monastery, perched on top called Jerusalem – a very good and obvious OP for the enemy.

The following day the remainder of the Regiment moved up to a concentration area near the bridge. Luckily Tim Readman had recced this place for he always picked a spot near or in a fig orchard so that we had plenty of fresh fruit until crossing the river in the evening.

The next day, C Squadron started to advance along the road to the west but were soon held up, so Timmie's troop was ordered to cut across country. Sgt Anderson's tank unfortunately was knocked out, killing one of the crew, whilst Sgt Anderson, who lost both legs, was taken prisoner with another of his crew. Timmie's tank was hit by an explosive 20mm whilst he was talking to a Gunner OP officer who was standing on the back of the tank. Timmie was hit in the ear and the Gunner was never seen again, except for the bits and pieces on Timmie's clothes. Sgt McHarg did some remarkably good rapid HE shooting as covering fire whilst Timmie pulled out.

The next morning an early advance was ordered as, owing to the darkness the previous night, it had been postponed. C Squadron led the advance and complete chaos started to reign, as during the night the wireless frequencies had changed but Massey thought it far easier to stick to the old one with the result that no one could get C Squadron on the air for quite a while. No serious opposition was met till the junction of Routes 6 and 7 – one coded as 'Fosse Way', the other 'Watling Street', and the Junction rather naturally 'Fosswat'. At this point one Battalion of Queens was to go along each road with two troops of A Squadron in support of each. The two troops on the right had to advance through olive orchards which gave very bad observation from the turret and they soon ran into a lot of trouble. Well-concealed tanks and guns knocked out three of our tanks. Graham Plews, along with two of his crew, was killed; Duggie's tank was hit in the differential which, for some reason, put it into reverse gear and the tank went slowly back, the driver being unable to put it into neutral or to switch off; it eventually came to rest in a ditch. Sgt McMeekin's tank was hit but still able to give valuable assistance by fire, whilst Sgt Jack's tank was bogged, so he dismounted his crew and Browning guns and, taking up a position, gave a lot of help till his ammunition ran out.

The Colonel and I had a first-class view of the battle from the top of a house at Fosswat. When we went back there the next day we found it demolished.

The other two troops on the left had gone as far as the small river of Lanzi which they were unable to cross as the bridge was blown. However, they assisted the infantry across and helped them to form a bridgehead so that the Sappers could put up a Bailey bridge.

The enemy were very fond of mounting a gun at the end of these long straight roads and firing at vehicles in the distance. Brigadier Lyne, commanding 169 Brigade, was up in his jeep one day and had parked it in front of Massey's, which Jackie Pert was driving, when the enemy opened up down the road and knocked the Brigadier's jeep out. Pert, very naturally, had jumped into the ditch and when he emerged again to get the jeep, he saw the Brigadier dressed in an extraordinary camouflaged helmet, driving away with it, so he shouted 'Oi, that's the Lord Roborough's jeep. You can't take it without his permission. Out you get.' They soon made friends and Jackie gave the Brigadier a lift back.

RHQ was set up in a graveyard amongst some trees, well hidden from the enemy, and B Squadron were just behind across the road. Everything was reasonably quiet until 169 Brigade decided to bring the whole of Main Brigade HQ into the woods opposite, to get into which the enemy had a clear view of all the caravans, ACVs etc., and, sure enough, shells started to come down, one of which landed beside Seymour Pears's tank, a splinter went into his back whilst he was sleeping and he died within minutes. I was awakened by SSM Dodd arriving in RHQ in an awful state, to get a doctor, but he was too late and no one would have been able to save him. This was a bitter blow to the Regiment as Seymour was beloved by all – officers and other ranks – and his burial by Padre Mac was a sad affair attended by the whole of B Squadron and all officers that were available. The amount of wild flowers put on his grave by his many friends was indeed touching and evidence of his popularity.

RHQ and C Squadron were behind an old farmhouse in this area listening to how A Squadron was doing in its attack along the road when shells started to drop round about till they eventually landed on the house. The next few minutes must have looked very funny from the air, as one by one the vehicles – jeeps, tanks, dingos, half-tracks – shot out from the buildings like bolted rabbits and made their way to a small wood.

It was near here that Massey came back to his Squadron very excited after a squadron leader's conference and told his troop leaders that there were forty enemy tanks in a certain area. Peter Paj tried to explain to him that it must be wrong as that area was behind our lines. However, Massey was not to be put off and said, 'No, the Colonel quite definitely said that forty tanks were there. I saw it on his map and copied it exactly.' Peter still wouldn't believe it so went to find out and it turned out to be the 40th Royal Tank Regiment, abbreviated to 40 Tanks!

The next role for the Regiment was to cross the Rio di Lanzi and, together with a Battalion of Queen's, capture the high ground over-looking the Savone di Riardo. A crossing of the Lanzi River had been recced by the Colonel and Ted Rob so that the tanks would not draw fire on the Bailey bridge which had just been erected. However, only one tank got across the stream before the second one got securely bogged. B Squadron, whose tank was stuck, remained there and event-ually got it out and the remainder across, whilst the rest of the Regiment went across the bridge. A Squadron finished up the day near Calvi Risorta where they were unfortunately shelled by a Defensive Fire (DF) task from our own Gunners, knocking out two tanks and wounding one man. It took some time to stop this fire, as no one would admit doing it. B Squadron in the meantime, had become mountaineers and road-builders, for Alec had got his troop up a very steep gully to a saddle on top of the feature, necessitating cutting away banks and building a track.

The next day showed lack of liaison between lower and higher formations, for all Squadrons were ordered to advance, which they did without opposition, although there was no sign of the infantry on the feature reported captured. Two hours after the Squadrons had reached their objectives and the information had been passed back, an order direct from GOC 56th Division was received to the effect that one troop of C Squadron was to support 44 Recce Regiment onto their objective. Great was Division's surprise when we replied that the place had already been captured two hours ago by A Squadron who were now two miles in front of it.

The Regiment had a rest for the next few days and were able to do some well-overdue maintenance on the tanks; various troops were on a few hour's notice to move in the event of the infantry being counter-attacked in front. These few days were spent at Sparanise or 'Robin's Ankles' as Colonel Lugs called it.

The Division was joined at this period by 168 Brigade who had come up from Sicily. They consisted of a Battalion of each of the following Regiments: London Scottish, Royal Ulster Rifles and Royal Berks – and were commanded by Brigadier Davidson. They arrived with a good reputation and certainly lived up to it, being a pleasure to work with instead of the other two Brigades. The Battalion of Royal Berks was commanded by that grand old warrior, Colonel Baird, whom we saw much of after the end of the War when he commanded a large military government area around Luneburg in Germany where we were stationed in 1947. He unfortunately died there.

The Colonel and I visited 168 Brigade HQ shortly after they arrived and they were in a most charming private house. Mansion houses in this poor part of Italy were few and far between and this was the only nice one I saw the whole time. That same day, the Colonel took me on a recce on foot in front of the A Squadron positions. We passed through a vineyard of the most delicious grapes and I got a terrific rocket when I started to pick and eat some, as just through the hedge was the main road which the enemy were supposed to be using. We never saw any, which was all to the good, for, as usual, neither of us were armed!

CHAPTER XVII

Savone di Riardo to the Garigliano

When 2/7 Queens put in their attack across the Savone di Riardo early on the morning of 19 October, there was supposed to be a ford between Montanaro – the Queen's base – and the other side of the river which the Regiment were expected to cross. Hugh Brassey recced this the day before and found it unsuitable but the Sappers decided they could lay a scissors bridge for the tanks and a small Bailey bridge for the light stuff. This bridge was ready at 7 a.m. and Alec's troop went across but found that the sunken lane leading up from the crossing was too narrow, so two companies of Queens were put on to widen it, which they did very speedily. Alec's troop and the forward infantry debouched from the lane at last light and leaguered just short of the railway.

The following day Alec started off at first light and moved straight to the Teano road where he was soon joined by the remainder of B Squadron. His and Hilary's troops then moved up to the Tranzi feature to assist the Ox and Bucks who were on it. A Squadron followed B Squadron across the main stream and were then directed to the left to support 8 RF's attack on Pugliano and Borgo. They had difficulty in finding a way across the small river Pescara – coded by Colonel Lugs to 'the pill' – however, they eventually got nine tanks across which did good work in the attack on the village.

Early that morning Colonel Lugs and I, on foot, crossed the railway which was our forward line to ask some farmers the whereabouts of the enemy, who were thought to have gone. This was 'Esther's Farm', where we spent the next week or so. We stopped behind a hedge to do our morning duty, being none too happy doing it in front of our forward troops for we would indeed have been caught 'with our trousers down' if an enemy had appeared.

A Squadron had difficulty in advancing the next day owing to the nature of the terrain – terraced slopes up the sides of the hills. The

Colonel and I visited them and, with Bob Hicks,[1] we found a way up to a higher road, whither the latter got his troop at the expense of losing a track. The Brigadier, seeing the difficulties we were having in the hills, ordered B Squadron to return to RHQ and A Squadron to concentrate between S. Marco and Pugliano. There was a blown bridge just short of S. Marco which Duggie tried to make crossable by breaking down the ends so the tanks could run down to the bottom on the rubble and up again. This he attempted by placing some charges in the bank and laying a line of petrol away from it for a hundred yards or so as a fuse. We arrived just in time to see him light it, but the flame never got right along.

The villages here were small with steep streets and quaint houses; clustered in one village was a company of pack mules manned by Mauritians, who, with their dark faces, seemed to tone in with the landscape.

A Squadron were held up at one place by a blown bridge but after a scout around by Recce Troop carriers a small cart-bridge was found which had been prepared for demolition. Whilst they were trying to get the charges out, the Colonel and I took a walk forward to the next road where we found some excited Italians who told us that there were three 'Tedescis'[2] asleep in a cave. Once again we were not armed so he sent me back for a weapon of sorts from A Squadron in the field behind. Before I got back, the Germans had been roused, so the Colonel advanced boldly towards them with his pipe pointing at them. They immediately surrendered and were useful in removing the charges from the bridge.

A and B Squadrons and RHQ spent the next ten days quietly in the Tranzi–S. Marco area as the infantry were now in the hills ahead which were impassable to tanks. RHQ were at Esther's Farm where Esther, the daughter, used to look after us well in the way of laundry and roast chestnuts, and used to make up to Colonel Lugs, being the 'big noise'! One day she came round the tanks collecting fallen acorns for the pigs and Frank strode up in a lordly fashion and drove her away saying, 'My dear girl, you can't do that here. Away, away.' The Colonel saw

---

1 Lieutenant R.E. Hicks, Troop Leader.
2 Germans

this all going on from the Orderly Room truck and shouted at her to come back and said to Frank, 'That's my girl. You can't turn her away.' Frank slunk off much to Colonel Lugs's amusement.

C Squadron, during all this time, had been attached to 168 Brigade who were advancing through Teano and on up the road to Roccamonfina. There were many bridges down and 'blows' in the road and they had difficulty in keeping up, having so many long halts whilst Sapper work was carried out. They reached the Roccamonfina area on 3 November and remained there for a few days ready to move on. They tried to get to Sippicciano which was the other side of Monte S. Croce but there was no route passable. On the 7th, however, they went round the south and west sides of the hill and got to the Clemente–Galluccio area without any trouble, where they were able to support the attack by 201 Guards Brigade on the Monte Camino feature which had started the night before. The Colonel and I had gone up to 201 Brigade HQ on the forward slope of Monte Croce in a chestnut forest to watch the attack starting after dark. It was a marvellous sight seeing all the shells bursting and tracers flying. It was on these occasions that the two sacks of chestnuts and apples which we always kept in the jeep proved so useful. The Guards lost heavily in this attack, and had many casualties from frostbite on top of this feature. Their chief objective was a small monastery on top (not Monte Cassino) but they never got there. They were able to consolidate on 'Razor Back Ridge' but supplying them was too difficult a job and they had to withdraw later.

On 11 November A and B Squadrons and RHQ moved up to this area and billeted in the small village of Fontana Fredda. The Colonel and Peter B went on ahead to recce B Squadron troop positions on the road overlooking the Garigliano between Ponte and S. Carlo. It was the first time that the Colonel did not take me with him and when I arrived at our new area I was to consider myself lucky as I saw the Colonel hobbling around all hunched up in a furious temper looking for his jeep. He and Peter had trodden on a 'S' mine and both had been hit in the legs, back and arms. These mines spring three feet into the air when triggered and then explode. They were both evacuated via 14 CCS to 92nd General Hospital in Naples. It was at first thought that they would only be about three weeks but a great blow came to the Regiment on 25 November when it was learnt that Colonel Lugs had died from the effects of jaundice on top of his wounds. This was a sad day for the Regiment for the Colonel was loved, admired and respected by all in the Regiment, and no finer officer had ever been in it.

Tim Readman immediately took command and Hugh took over B Squadron. These two continued the recce for the Squadron positions which were occupied after dark. Fontana Fredda was in a valley running into a shoulder of Monte Croce and there was only one ridge between it and the B Squadron positions. It was on top of this ridge that Frank found positions for A Squadron to occupy if necessary. Otherwise the Squadron lay up beside RHQ.

The Regiment remained in this area for a week during most of which time there was incessant rain. C Squadron drew back from the front line and concentrated in an area near Sippicciano which soon turned into a quagmire. One night an enemy patrol got very close to them but no damage was done. The tanks were practically inextricable so it was lucky they did not have a hurried move. After the second day's rain all the temporary bridges on the Ponte road were washed away, so Tim and I went round the other way to the small village of Vescara and had a very pleasant walk over the hill and through orchards to C Squadron who were very surprised to see us arriving on foot from the wrong direction. The Squadron remained in this area until 26 November.

B Squadron remained in their positions till 24 November and spent this time observing enemy movements across the river from OPs. They got the routine of the various enemy posts carefully worked out and they used to have great fun laying on the latrine and firing whenever someone came out of a dugout – the shell arriving the same time as the man!

RHQ were very well off in their village and I shared a room with Charlie Radclyffe, John Warrender and Carlo Civitella, an Italian Liaison Officer who had just been posted to us. There was a very nice family in the house – simple peasants, and they used to bring us wine and chestnuts roasting on a charcoal fire in a bucket.

I had a lovely walk one afternoon with Tim over the hill in front to B Squadron. There was a superb view from the top – the sea to the left, Gaeta peninsula, the mass of Monte Aurunci across the front and then Monte Cassino with the monastery glistening on the right. The day before we left this village we discovered that our delightful family had stolen a lot of kit from members of RHQ – torches, clothing and other personal items – so we were glad to be away.

Carlo was a marvellous person; he was quite old, about forty, and very prim. The first night, after putting on his silk pyjamas, he proceeded to wrap his feet up in *The Times* which he declared, kept his feet warm – the *Daily Herald*, of course, was no good! After the first day or so, he soon became one of us and we used to pull his leg continually. He was an Italian Duke and a great friend of the Crown Prince; often he would get back in the evening having had a meal with him and full of the latest news. We made a collection of 'Carlo-isms' – expressions used by him. The following are but a few – a tonner, a three-tonner; a yip, a jeep; a behavy, a beehive, and many other amusing ones. One day he was at Corps HQ dressed in his funny little Italian officers' side-hat, when General Dick McCreery passed. He did a little bow of his head and doffed his hat; then he got in an awful state that he hadn't saluted for 'My God, and who it was, it was the Corps Commander.' He had a limp and used to walk with a stick and very sedate and stiff strides, but he was mad keen to go on a patrol down to the river. He remained with us till we left Italy and he became a very great friend of ours. His mother was a Scotswoman so he was half-British.

On 18 November orders were received that RHQ, Recce Troop and A Squadron were to return to Tranzi for three weeks to train with 201 Guards Brigade so the next day we all moved back and arranged leave parties in Naples. We took a building for a leave hostel and it was all ready to start with John Warrender in charge when on the 23rd we were ordered to move up to the river again so all the leave business was cancelled. On the 24th we moved to an area two miles SW of Sessa Aurunca and B Squadron moved to the village of Lauro about four miles away, where they were to support 11 KRRC, commanded by Colonel Chris Consett. On the 26th C Squadron came to the farm next to RHQ and at last were able to get under cover after spending three miserable weeks in pelting rain in a quagmire. Their new home was unfortunately under observation from the hills across the river so they had to be careful. The first night of rain, Peter Paj and David got up, stood at their windows and revelled at the fact that it was raining and they were dry.

I have already referred to the great loss the Regiment suffered with the death of Colonel Lugs Fiennes on 25 November. Tim Readman that same day twisted his ankle badly and cracked a small bone so had to have his leg and foot encased in plaster. This prevented him from attending the funeral the following day.

On the 27th and 29th, RHQ and Recce Troop areas were shelled by a high-velocity gun. The shell burst and a second of so later you could hear the gun firing. One of our soldiers Tpr Batchelor, was talking to a military policeman outside Brigade HQ, which was next door, and both were killed by one of these shells. Hugh was visiting Brigade HQ at the same time and when he came out of the ACV he found his jeep on fire having been hit.

On St Andrews Day – 30 November – I went to recce a range area by the sea at the foot of Monte Massico. It was a large area of reclaimed land on the seaward side of the Via Appia. This range was used periodically until B Squadron were firing there on 12 December when the enemy started to shell them, so they made a hurried exit and the range was not used again.

A and B Squadron each undertook a small operation in this area. On 1 December, B Squadron supported an attack by 11 KRRC on certain enemy-held houses our side of the river so as to draw the enemy's attention from the impending large-scale attack by 46th and 56th Divisions on Monte Camino. The Squadron's object was to make bogus wireless messages representing an attack over the river and formation of a bridgehead. This was done by troop leaders from Dingo scout cars. The scheme was highly successful as was found out by intercepts which showed that great alarm and despondency was raised in 94 German Infantry Division.

Duggie Stewart took one of his troops out to a position short of the river to engage enemy targets, chiefly houses used as OPs. This was done with the object of practising tank commanders on correction of fire at ranges between five and seven thousand yards. Dick Kirk was also there and allowed some of them to fire his battery of Priests which had been attached to us for the last two months.

There was an infantry battalion in the next village of Carano whom

I used to visit occasionally as RIO. This village was typically Italian and in the middle was a charming old white-washed villa where Battalion HQ was. It had an archway into a courtyard where there was every sort of creeper and shrub. Inside, there were some lovely rooms with velvet curtains, painted ceilings, good pictures and furniture. It belonged to a rich doctor, I think, and it was marvellous sitting down to tea in the dining room – it made one forget anything about a war or that the enemy were only a few miles off.

The house where we lived, on the other hand, was an amazing place. Downstairs was a sitting room where Tim, Frank and Ru slept, and upstairs, in a room which was half an attic and through which civilians had to go to get to the lavatory, John Warrender, Richard Shelley, Charlie Radclyffe, Carlo Civitella and myself slept and ate; and several times had to put up someone else who was spending the night at RHQ. The owner of the house was a mental woman and Carlo and she used to stand in the room and scream at each other.

There was a great excitement on 10 December as an order was received that the Regiment would hand over all the tanks to 50 Royal Tank Regiment in the next few days, rejoin 4th Armoured Brigade in Eighth Army and go home to prepare for the Second Front. As is usual with all such orders, this was postponed as 50 RTR could not be spared from Eighth Army for another month. So instead of going home to Scotland we got orders to go 'home' to Tranzi where we had been already twice before and which was about ten miles behind. B Squadron moved there on the 13th just as RHQ was being rather heavily shelled. The remainder of the Regiment moved the following day.

Whilst we had been in this place most people had gone for their three days' Naples leave. I went with Peter Paj, and Hilary Marshall. We went back via Peter Has and B Echelon where we were fortified for our journey – ever since moving to the desert in 1942, every officer going on leave had done this. Peter, as always, was well established in a small house in Casanova with Tony B. Ted Acres used to live in his caravan in the olive grove behind, and his address was 'The Caravan, Casanova Woods'! We had rented a nice flat in Naples for the officers to spend their leave in and it turned out to be very useful. We had great fun and did a lot of shopping. There were several good shops and in one we found a Briggs umbrella and a Locks bowler! There were one or two excellent restaurants where you could have a good, expensive, black-market meal. The best was the Zie Therese which was under the promenade overlooking the Bay. In the evenings we used to go to the 'Orange Grove', a nightclub on the hill very well run by the Americans. One day we went to Pompeii and saw the ruins which were incredible – so old yet so well-preserved by the dust that had covered them from Vesuvius. We had a horrible drive back to the Regiment at night and had to take a diversion along some narrow roads which we didn't know. At one place we were more or less lost so got out and stopped a car to ask the way. This turned out to be Brigadier Harry Arkwright who was also lost!

One of the pleasures of an armoured regiment was living 'on one's tank', i.e. all ranks 'mucked in' on the vehicle, sleeping beside it, sharing the cooking and the food. The crews of Astra (my tank) and Aux (the Colonel's) messed together along with Millar (the jeep driver) and Sgt O'Rourke (the Dingo driver). We were a pleasant and jolly lot and the crew were very kind to us for so often the Colonel and I in either the jeep or Dingo were out for most of the day and the remainder would always ensure there was something ready for us on our return. When we could, we helped with the cooking – but our more welcome contribution was additions to the rations which we collected from various farms on our trips. Sgt O'Rouke was a splendid person to have around and to be out with in the Dingo.

CHAPTER XVIII

Waiting to go home

When we arrived in our new area on 14 December, we were told we would be there over Christmas for a period of Brigade Training, but in actual fact it was to prepare our tanks before handing them over to 50 RTR and then proceeding home. The Regiment was split up in various farms along the Teano road near Tranzi. Our mess in RHQ was two rooms in a small farmhouse on the edge of a wooded gully and to get to it you had to go across a burn by a wooden plank, which was under water after rain. It was really a very attractive place. One room was a mess with wooden benches and the other room was for Colonel Tim, Frank and Ru to sleep in. Charlie Radclyffe, Carlo and myself slept in an EPIP tent pitched between two haystacks outside.

The furniture in our mess was three wooden forms, two tables and one or two wooden chairs – not very comfortable. We had a stove put in which made it a bit warmer and at dinner at night we put a blanket over the table which, draped to the floor and an oil stove underneath it, kept our legs very warm.

One rainy day, David set out to look for wood to make a dining hall for A Squadron, and he soon found some in a sawmill, but when he started to remove it the owner came rushing up to him gesticulating. David realized that he wanted a signature so scribbled on a piece of paper which satisfied him. A few days later a message came from Division demanding the presence of the officer who left a note in a sawmill saying 'Fucking wet day today; back tomorrow'. This was obviously David who had to see Lieutenant Colonel Hall, the A/Q, about it. When he arrived he was told to sit in the armchair in the A/Q's caravan as 'you might as well be comfortable whilst I give you a rocket.' David said it was the toughest rocket he ever had and sitting in the low armchair with Colonel Hall towering above him made him feel very small.

During our stay here we did many schemes and TEWTs (Tactical Exercise Without Troops). The Squadrons gave demonstrations of cross-country performance, camouflage, parachute flares etc., but they were usually spoilt by pelting rain and most of the tanks got bogged. When we got time off many of us went shooting. There were two areas only that were any good: one was in the hills behind Tranzi where there were a few woodcock and pigeons, and the other place was the marshes at Castel Volturno by the mouth of the river. Here there were any amount of duck and a few snipe. We used to have some good days there, most of our bag being green plover which appeared in hordes and made surprisingly good eating.

Charlie was walking past the Recce Troop vehicles one day and saw someone who, he imagined, was a new officer, very smartly dressed in a pair of American overalls, so he had a long talk with him and introduced himself. When he saw John Warrender, he asked him who the new officer was, 'whom I've had a long chat to, old boy; damn nice fellow, what!' This turned out to be Trooper 'Flash' Gordon; Charlie didn't know quite what to do!

We were lucky again that year in being out of the line at Christmas so we were able to have a reasonably good time. As usual the rations for Christmas Dinner were excellent and everyone had a thoroughly good feed after Padre Mac had held a service which was well attended in the large Recreation Tent at B Echelon.

On the 18th, Frank became our first officer malarial casualty and he was evacuated to hospital. Probably no one was keener over taking his Mepachrine than Frank, yet he was the only one to get this disease.

On Hogmanay, it never stopped pelting and the large tent, where the customary Sergeants' Mess smoker was being held, got more and more leaks so that the ground inside became a sea of mud and many duck-boards had to be laid. However, the party went off extremely well with Mr Anderton, the RSM, in charge. Shortly after midnight a terrible gale blew up – reputed to be the worst in Italy within living memory. The large tent half collapsed and everyone struggled to bed. Alwyne had taken over as Adjutant and was in our tent which we reached about 2.30. At 3.30 the tent blew down on top of us so Carlo and I salvaged what we could and struggled into the farm kitchen to finish off the night. Besides a gale there was driving sleet and we tried to make Alwyne come with us but the tent was lying on top of him, keeping him dry, so he preferred to stay. We were soon woken up again by hammering on the door which turned out to be Alwyne who couldn't stand it any longer, an extra strong gust of wind having blown the tent away and flattened one of the haystacks over just where we had been sleeping. We spent the next morning salvaging books, trousers, shirts etc. from the burn at the bottom of the gully. Our Miles-Neilson (earth closet) had been placed at a discreet distance away from the mess – 100 yards – in the middle of a field and it was most uncomfortable, to put it mildly, using it that day.

I went on a very interesting trip one day to the Americans near Mignano, via Roccamonfina and a lot of little side roads, trying to trace a certain tank Regiment which I never found. Everyone was very kind in helping me and I eventually got the new gun manual I wanted from another unit. The country round there was very attractive, the hills much steeper and bolder; most of the villages were built on sides of hills or ravines and usually had an old castle or monastery in them. Going through one small village, I passed a truckload of Scots Guards at the side of the road. The officer with them turned out to be Iain Moncreiffe, who was a great friend of mine – it is extraordinary how small the world is. I came back from this trip by Route 6 – the main road.

Several days were spent on the range at the eastern side of Monte Massico. I went with A Squadron on a marvellous sunny day and we had great fun firing at various targets on the hill.

Although no one had been told that we were going home, it was taken for granted by most people and on 15 January General McCreery came himself to say goodbye to the officers and NCOs of the Regiment and to thank us for the vital part we had played in the operations from Salerno to the Garigliano. At Salerno, he said, it was entirely due to the Regiment that X Corps were not thrown off the beaches. Another nice tribute to the Regiment's vital work at Salerno was paid by Major General Graham, GOC 56th Division at the landings. In forwarding a donation to the Regimental War Memorial Fund, he said:

> At the Salerno Landing, when I commanded 56th Division, I was indeed fortunate to have to work with my division such a grand Regiment as the Greys. I shall never forget all they did at the time. There were some anxious moments but all was well in the end. That it was so, was largely

due to the steadfastness and indomitable spirit of your Regiment. There are many glorious episodes in your history but what you did at Salerno will bear comparison with any.

On 14 January 50 RTR arrived to bivouac in our area till we had handed over our vehicles to them. The next few days were spent in doing this and we played them at football one day and won 9-0. On the 19th the whole Regiment, in RASC transport, left for a new area just outside Naples, preparatory to embarking.

The Regiment was split in half – RHQ and A Squadron in a large villa in Afragola and B and C Squadron in a schoolhouse in Casoria, about two miles away. Our villa was a pleasant spot with large airy rooms, a courtyard and a garden. As is usual in most Italian houses, there were no WCs so Miles-Neilsons were made everywhere in the garden. We were here for a week and everyone got immensely excited. The general smartness improved beyond all measure, because the men were prepared to do anything as they were going home.

From here we went on sightseeing trips to Vesuvius and Pompeii. I went with a party to the former place one day, taking our lunch with us. The trucks took us past the observatory nearly to the top so we only had about half an hour zig-zag walk up the last steep bit. It was an incredible sight on top, for red molten lava was bubbling out of the earth and the rocks were too hot to stand on in thin shoes. There were men there who made ashtrays out of lava for you if you produced a coin, round which they would mould it and then let it cool off. We all climbed farther up to the rim of the crater and looked down into an inferno of smoke and weird noises. Every now and again there would be a small 'woomph' and a few bits of earth would shoot up. It was evidently, at the time, working up for its big eruption two months later. We had an awful time coming down to the lorries as everyone went straight down instead of keeping to the zig-zag path. The surface was loose shingle with an occasional boulder and halfway down two men – one of them, Tpr Dalziel ('Dazzle') – tripped and started to run. It was so steep and the surface so loose they couldn't stop and got faster and faster, as in a nightmare, until at last they caught their toes on a stone and dived head first down, their heads being the first things to hit the ground where there happened to be boulders. Why they weren't killed, I don't know; they only had badly cut heads. We had to carry them down the rest of the way, bind them up and then drop them at the hospital on the way back. Luckily for them, they were fit enough to sail with us the following week.

The Naples Opera Company had started again and many of us went in to see them..The S. Carlo was a fine Opera House, next door to the Officers' Club, and part of the Royal Palace. The singing, dresses and music were superb and we were indeed lucky to have been able to see these Italian operas acted in Naples.

We made great friends with a very unpleasant war-profiteering, Swiss-Italian wine merchant in Naples called Hans Jenni. He was very useful in being able to supply an endless variety of liqueurs and wines, but he thought of nothing but his pocket and put the prices up to a rich-sounding Regiment. In the end he lost money with us hand over fist. He was certain that the lira would crash, so wanted sterling, and as he had an account with a Swiss bank in London, he asked us all to pay his bills by cheque to his bank in London, leaving him a duplicate. He also volunteered to cash cheques for us. When we got home we all sent our cheques off but were told they couldn't be paid to his account as he was in an enemy country or some reason like that. So none of us paid a thing. Some fifteen years later he caught up with us with the help of the *Daily Express* whose headlines were: 'Bubbly jocks owe money to Italian wine merchant!'

There were a surprising amount of silk stockings and handkerchiefs in various shops but by the time we sailed there were not many left!

There were many good parties held at the Officers' Club in Naples before we left. The great thing was to buy up a lot of bottles of very cheap local champagne and shoot the corks, which popped out after shaking, at a woman singing with the band. She was a large buxom dame in a green dress, with on her chest a big brooch which was the bull's-eye. She didn't see the joke. But an old General sitting at a table the other side of the room onto whom we traversed and gave 'ten rounds gunfire' thought it was very funny.

We spent the 25th frantically packing, as all heavy baggage had to be sent to the docks the next day and Colonel Joe Dudgeon, who was commanding a pack-mule Transport Regiment, came to say goodbye to us before we left.

On the 27th we all set off on foot to march to the docks. It was a good five miles, but nobody seemed to mind how far they marched with home at the end of it. We had a dispersal area in a street where we had sandwiches and waited four hours.

During this time people went off to get a final supply of wines from Hans Jenni, for we heard that our ship was 'dry'. We also found the Naples equivalent to 'Groppi' or 'Charbonnel and Walker' and bought most of their stock. We were eventually called forward and embarked on the Dutch ship SS *Tegelburg* by seven in the evening.

CHAPTER XIX

The Journey Home

A fter going on board, there was complete chaos as everyone got lost in the passages and decks and no one knew the way to his own part of the ship, but somehow it got sorted out and we sat down, exhausted, to a meal. We left Naples at half past eight on the morning of 28 January 1944 and the convoy went straight across to the coast of Africa which we sighted at Bizerta the following day. The next day we sighted Algiers, whence four ships joined our convoy and we passed another large convoy of fifty ships going in the opposite direction. The next day Oran was sighted and several ships from our convoy left to go there. That afternoon we spotted the snow-capped Sierra Nevada Hills on the Spanish mainland and the Isle of Alboran on our port beam. That evening at dark the convoy changed formation to double line and fixed the anti-mine paravanes prior to passing through the Straits of Gibraltar, which was done at midnight when we saw the lights of Spain and Tangiers on either beam.

After one rough day we had perfect weather all through the Mediterranean and we sat out on the deck in the sun, for after muster parade at ten o'clock for the Captain's inspection there was nothing else to do. I shared one of the state cabins with five others and there was a spare bunk for each of us so we had plenty of room to spread ourselves. The food as usual on these boats was very good but the big drawback was no drink, although it was surprising how much must have been brought on by individual officers. Peter Has had a good supply and there were parties in his cabin most nights. We spent most of the time playing chess, pacing the deck for exercise or sitting in the sun on fine days.

On the ship were HQ 4th Armoured Brigade, 3 CLY, ourselves and a few oddments. Everyone was in very good spirits and soon everybody knew everybody, if not to talk to, anyway to nod to. There was a very good shop on board where one could buy things like decent soap and scent to take home as presents.

On the morning of 1 February the hills of Spain finally disappeared over the horizon and so we saw no land till the 7th when Northern Ireland was sighted; then soon appeared, in order, the Mull of Kintyre, Ayrshire, Isle of Arran and Ailsa Craig, all before midday. We dropped anchor off Rothesay in the afternoon, once more in Scottish waters. We were to have disembarked the following day, but owing to lack of rolling stock, this was not done till the 10th. The 8th was spent steaming slowly up the Clyde past Gourock, Greenock, Port Glasgow and Dumbarton till we berthed at Shield Hall Dock. The whole way up the river there were crowds of dockers lining the quays cheering us home; the only reply they got from the men on board were very sarcastic remarks about dock strikes. Hugh no longer had to sing 'Sailing up the "humm"', for it was no longer a secret!

On the last day without seeing land, we had a ship's concert which was very ably compared by Sgt 'Harvey' Naylor who was always the life and soul of any regimental concert. His trick towards the end, of playing a roll of drums and then 'King Farouk' (a rousing tune with typical soldier-language words added), worked perfectly on the old Captain who thought it was the National Anthem and jumped up to try and say a few words before it started. Another excellent turn done by the Regiment was Alwyne and Denis acting the Western Brothers.

The 9th was spent with Customs officials who behaved admirably. They had all the men in the big mess deck and told them they were allowed so many cigarettes, etc. and then asked if anyone had more than that; one man said he had and was immediately told by the Customs man to count them again, for he was surely wrong! They never attempted to charge anyone for anything. I had about eighteen silk handkerchiefs and when I declared them, he said 'That's alright. A present I presume.' He never gave me time even to say 'yes', but passed me by. They were evidently very good to any troops returning from foreign service; the people they were out to catch were the ship's permanent staff, and I believe they caught our ship's RSM and RQMS who had cigarettes hidden all round their cabin.

On 10 February 1944, the Royal Scots Greys set foot once again in Scotland after an absence from that country of nine years.

We were not to stay long in Scotland for we were soon on a train for Worthing and were in England by midday. We had a long and tiring journey and arrived after midnight. NAAFI fed us at several halts on the journey and 88 A/Tk Regiment were at Worthing Station to meet us. They had fires lit in every room and a hot meal waiting and we were indeed grateful to them. We got to bed that night tired but contented and excited at the idea of once more being home again.

The entire Regiment broke up on leave during the next two days except for a holding staff of John Parkin,[1] Ted Acres and twenty-nine ORs. Everyone got a week's leave plus a week for every year abroad – maximum being a month.

It was indeed extraordinary to be home again, seeing English people in the streets, English cars on the road, and everything else. Duggie gave his taxi driver a most awful rocket for driving on the wrong side of the road – or so he thought after five and a half years of driving on the other side!

---

[1] Lieutenant J. Parkin, Troop Leader.

PART III – NORTH-WEST EUROPE

CHAPTER XX

Preparing for Normandy

As soon as everyone had returned to Worthing from leave, training for the 'Second Front' started in earnest – at least in as much earnest as equipment would allow, for tanks and B vehicles had to be drawn from all over England, which took some weeks. Towards the end of March, the Sabre Squadrons went to fire on a large tank range near Kirkcudbright and were away for a week.

Two new troops were formed here – AA Troop, and Recce Troop equipped with Stuart tanks. The former had Crusader tanks with double Oerlikon guns mounted in a roofless turret. Although I was in the newly-formed Recce Troop, I had to take the AA Troop on a course to Lulworth and ranges in Cumberland. On my return Bob Grey took over the Troop and I rejoined Recce of which John Gunn was Troop Leader and John Althorp the other subaltern.

Our four months in Worthing were taken up by schemes, at home or away, visits and inspections. The training area was in the Downs behind and we had great fun doing Recce Troop training which often entailed spending the night out, but we had good weather and everyone enjoyed themselves. We did many schemes with the Highland Division at Worthing and most of our officers went to Cambridgeshire for a large exercise laid on by them.

Several old Greys visited the Regiment informally, including Colonel Touche Gaisford St Lawrence, Colonel Doodie Pigot Moodie and Roland Findlay. Field Marshal Chetwode, our Colonel, paid an official visit to us and our Brigadier, John Currie, welcomed us back into 4th Armoured Brigade by an inspection, address and march past. General Dempsey, Army Commander, paid a visit and walked round the Regiment. Then in May, General Montgomery, 21 Army Group Commander, inspected the Brigade and spoke to everyone from his customary perch, the bonnet of a jeep. He would not tell us exactly what our job was going to be but he said that we would not be asked to do anything that we had not done before.

No one knew when the invasion was going to be, and everyone led a day-to-day existence, which, on the whole, was quite enjoyable for the weather was good and some of us played golf every evening after tea – the Mess being conveniently situated on the course. Peter Paj and Richard Shelley, who became Adjutant in April, had two or three days hunting. London was very handy for unmarried officers and there were some shocking sights on the Milk Train on Monday mornings!

Although Worthing was in the coastal prohibited area, wives were allowed and there was a reasonable amount of gaiety. We gave a large sherry party in the garden at Skyrings, the Mess, and another large one was given by the Workshops at Castle Goring, which was a few miles away. Tony Bonham tells a very funny story about how he and Flick, Hugh and Joyce Brassey and Frank and Joan Bowlby went to this party in a 15cwt truck, strictly illegal for families; halfway back Frank got a very guilty conscience, made Joan get out and they walked the last two miles home!

The following officers who gained the Military Cross in the desert and Italy, together with some other ranks, attended an investiture at Buckingham Palace where the King presented their medals: Frank, Duggie, Peter Paj, Mo, Ted Rob and Timmie Parker.

As May drew to a close, we all reckoned that the second front would be starting any moment as special security precautions were taken and our heavy baggage was sent home. We still did not know our role and speculation was rife.

On 5 June, we were given definite orders to move to a concentration area near our port of embarkation the following morning at eight o'clock.

CHAPTER XXI

The Crossing

While we were enjoying our last evening in comfort and thinking how lucky we were at setting off at such a reasonable hour, a message came through to say we were to start at 4 a.m. which meant reveille at two. Everyone naturally began to flap and I got off to bed as soon as possible to get what sleep I could.

The start on the morning of 6 June went off surprisingly smoothly and the tanks all pulled out more or less on time. Many of those who spent the night out and had not heard of the change of time were seen catching us up all along the route. It was quite a nice morning and we had a lovely drive via Arundel, Chichester, and Petersfield to our marshalling area just outside Portsmouth. Soon after it got light we saw an incredible number of planes and gliders coming and going, so we guessed that the invasion had taken place and we were therefore not part of the Assault Force. On arrival everyone was split up into crafts and I was made craft commander which entailed contacting all vehicles that were with me, and I never seemed to stop running madly to and fro. We were now inside the security zone and our role was given out to us, maps issued and our money changed to French francs, so there was now no doubt where we were going to. Our role was to follow up the main assaulting divisions. The time of move was altered four times and we eventually got away at 10 p.m. to another area from which we were expected to be called forward any time to board our craft. We therefore never got any bedding down and I slept curled up like a dog on the engine cover of my tank.

The next morning everyone but ourselves seemed to move forward but our turn came at last at 11 a.m. when we drove down to the docks at Gosport and waited till 2 p.m. when we returned after receiving orders and counter-orders most of the time. It was very pleasant on the docks as it was a sunny day and we watched all sorts of vehicles being loaded up. An enormous mobile crane was halfway up the ramp onto an LCT when it started to run backwards out of control. The driver jumped clear into the sea and the crane then toppled over and lay half submerged. The rest of the day was peaceful; we had a good meal and were able to get our beds down for the night. The following morning we had a long lie-in and breakfasted peacefully on M & V stew and tinned peaches, which was our only food and did us every meal. The whole day was spent there and the owners of the houses on the road were exceedingly kind and let us in to wash and shave. We were all going to sleep in the houses as well but just as we were getting our bedding down, word was passed round for us to move back to the docks. On arrival we were told that there would be no craft that night and we were to pull off the docks and 'get down to it' which we did till 3 a.m. when we were roused and given orders to go to Southsea to embark on an LST as the plans had been changed.

We had an hour's wet and uncomfortable sleep at a halt and then moved on to a street where we breakfasted and remained till midday in the rain. We then slowly progressed towards the 'hards' and got on board the LST which pulled out at 3 p.m. to join the convoy in the Solent. It was fairly rough while we were riding at anchor but as soon as the convoy started at 8 p.m. it got smoother.

I had the best sleep since leaving Worthing – eight hours – and awoke to find ourselves about a mile off the coast of France in a maze of shipping. The sight in Salerno Bay was fairly amazing but nothing to equal this. Evidently during the night there had been 'action stations' when six enemy destroyers came in sight but nothing happened. We should have disembarked at 6 a.m. but we missed the tide so waited till ten when a LCU (Landing Craft Unloading), with an open back and front, arrived and the vehicles disembarked onto it; it was then able to get to the shore, landing us at about 2 p.m. near the village of Craye-sur-Mer.

CHAPTER XXII

Caen

I had about half of the Recce Troop on my ship and when we got ashore on 9 June we set off to the Regimental Collecting Area at Reviers. When we got there, not a sign of them could we see, so I went off in 'Glensax' (my tank) to look for them and eventually found them at a small village called Amblie, where we had a few hours rest and were able to have a brew and a wash. I was given a refreshing glass of milk, straight from the cow, by an old farmer. There was a very attractive small chateau here where 4th Armoured Brigade had their Headquarters and where Paul Reay,[1] our LO at Brigade, had been badly wounded by a Butterfly bomb the day he landed. At 8 p.m. we moved to the leaguer area at Le Fresne-Camilly. On arrival John Gunn and I went for a 'swan' in the 'Weasel'[2] to have a look at the surrounding country, and got back to bed at midnight.

Reveille the next day was at 4.30 and everything a bit hectic and flappish as everyone overslept – John Parkin was told by Colonel Tim that, if he couldn't wake up at reveille, he would have to stay awake all night! We eventually moved off to our positions at a quarter past five with a rocket.

After a nasty breakfast from a '24-hour pack', I was suddenly sent for to recce a route to Basly and in the afternoon the Regiment moved to a small village of Colomby-sur-Thaon which was not so very far from the underground strongpoint which, although surrounded, was still holding out. We remained in this place for ten days during which the Recce Troop was out on patrol every day from 4 a.m. till midnight, getting only two to three hours sleep. One day while sitting in my OP I saw David Callander in front of me. When I had another look, he wasn't there and I must have dreamed he was there while still awake and conscious. At times one got into that sort of condition through lack of sleep. We had very good positions where we watched the enemy

---

1 Lieutenant H.M.P. Reay.
2 A light tracked vehicle whose tracks could propel it in water.

in the villages of Gruchy and Villons-les-Buissons. There was a small wood where one of my sections was and it was full of very good wild strawberries. While at this place, I did a recce to Benouville and Ranville where Airborne Troops had captured the bridge over the River Orne. The country round the bridge was an amazing sight as it was littered with gliders and parachutes – there were so many gliders in such a small space that it was not unlike Ascot car park. I went with Major 'Cocky' Leakey (second in command of 44 RTR) and we visited Airborne Divisional HQ in a very nice chateau by Ranville and Para Brigade HQ where we were well received with a mug of whisky. When I got back to the Regiment, a lot of men were riding round the orchard on horses which they had found spare.

While we were at Colomby, there were many flaps when the enemy attacked or we were about to attack, and twice we were all ready to move over to the other side of the Orne when it was cancelled. On 21 June I led the Regiment along the route I had recced the previous day back to Le Fresne-Camilly. The route went through the grounds of a large chateau called Fontaine-Henry where the owner and his family were standing in the porch waving to us, with an old labrador lying at their feet – a nice peaceful sight.

We were told we would be there for a few days' rest which was pleasing news as, for the last fifteen days, I had averaged four hours sleep a day and was dead beat. We were in a large field surrounded by a hedge so, with the aid of the hedge, the tank and the tarpaulin, we made ourselves quite comfortable. In this field were the remains of the special fittings round the DD Tanks (the ones that swam ashore).

We remained here for five days during which we were able to do overdue maintenance and laundry. There was a little collection of farms called Cainet in the valley below where most of the Regiment went to in the evenings to buy eggs, milk, cream, butter and veal. They all seemed to be in ample abundance as I was allowed to buy five kilos of butter for my troop from one farm – or maybe it was because of 'la vieille alliance' (Scottish/French) of which I reminded them! While we were in this location, we had a lecture from an RTR officer on tank recognition. After the War this same officer was our Brigade G3 for nearly three years – Brian (Boomer) Watkins – and became a good friend of the Regiment.

On 26 June, after six hours' delay, we moved off for the forthcoming operation to break out from the beachhead. This objective was given every time there was an offensive, and one seldom got more than a mile of two. Our concentration area was Norrey-en-Bessin – known as Willoughby-in-the-bath! – and forward of this, beside the main Caen to Tilly-sur-Seulles road, the Regiment took up positions. A Squadron had gone through an unmarked minefield and lost two tanks. There was a small wood in our area where there were some snipers concealed and these turned out to number about forty and were soon captured. It was a bad day all round as our Brigadier, John Currie, had been killed, it pelted hard all evening and everyone was soaked and had to sleep in the tanks. Brigadier Mike Carver took over the Brigade that day at the age of twenty-nine and remained with it for nearly three years.

The following day I was sent across to Fontenay-le-Pesnil, commonly known as 'Piss in the Fountain', to contact 8th Armoured Brigade. On the way over, I had a first-class view of four Panther tanks coming out of a wood and being engaged and knocked out by the Regiment. I spent most of that day with the Sherwood Rangers in an orchard full of dead Germans, their bodies swollen and faces a horrible green, leaden colour. I visited their Commanding Officer, Stanley Christopherson, several times at his RHQ and the last time I was there, his forward squadron brought in two captured German tanks which he asked me to escort back. As the road along which I led them had been changing hands quite often I was none too happy in case some keen anti-tank gunner might let fly. On my way back to the Regiment, Cpl Randall and I had an amusing encounter with two Germans in a cornfield. I caught sight of them in the long corn and shouted at them to surrender. They promptly hid in the corn then bobbed up behind. We tried shooting at the places where we thought they were and running the tanks at them hoping they would give themselves up. They at last stood up and surrendered and when I tried to get out to search them, I got all tied up with my glasses, pistol, headset etc. and started to curse. How they must have laughed to themselves. I had seen so many dead bodies that day, that everything I saw on the way home appeared to be another one till I got up to it.

On 28 June the Regiment moved south of Cheux and I went on and recced a route to the River Odon via Colleville; 15th Scottish Division had made a thin corridor down the road to the river opposite Baron so the route was this small road with high banks either side. Everything possible went wrong on that trip. The road was packed with every sort of vehicle, like Piccadilly in the rush hour, and I had my ration box torn off by a lorry. Then Cpl Randall's tank got ditched but luckily a bulldozer was behind him which managed to pull him out, and to crown everything my engine conked out but again the gods were with me: an ARV happened to be passing and gave me a tow which eventually started the engine. I was thankful to get back in spite of finding the Regiment having a bit of a battle trying to keep this narrow corridor open against the threat of some enemy tanks.

The following day the Regiment was attached to 129 Brigade for an operation to clear the wooded area round Mouen as far as the river. My section was attached to Duggie (A Squadron) and, together with an infantry battalion, we advanced against very little opposition through thick country as far as the Odon which we could not cross so sat on a nice heather slope overlooking the river and had a good view of 11th Armoured Division's tank battle south of the river at Baron. As so often happens, on the way home down a very narrow lane, we were told to turn round and go back to take up positions as there was a flap. After a lot of manoeuvring the Squadron turned round only to be told it could come home after all. We were much amused over our infantry as this was evidently their first battle and they were doing everything according to the book: their faces were blackened; they had cut off all badges of rank; and they talked in whispers.

At three o'clock in the morning we were all woken as there was a flap on – 15th Scottish Division were being driven back from the river. The Recce Troop had to go to a certain crossroads and prepare to act as guides, so it was lucky that I had not taken any bedding down and slept in my clothes on the grass under my tank that night as I was so late getting back and it was raining so hard. This crossroads was about a mile away and I was not terribly sure of the track except that it passed a dead grey carthorse. The mud was about a foot deep and I started off plodding my way on foot in front of the tank. I was relieved when at last I smelt the horse and finally reached our destination. I was challenged many times but not shot at. We stayed at this spot about an hour and saw many infantry coming back before we were recalled as the enemy had been held.

Four-leaf clovers seemed to be a common plant in that part of France for I found several most days. In one small patch on the green in the village of Marcelet overlooking Carpiquet Aerodrome I found seven.

On 7 July I visited units of the Guards Division and had a very social day meeting several friends, for at the Coldstream Battalion HQ I found Sandy Stratheden commanding and Charles Lambton as Adjutant; while at the Welsh Guards, Charlie Radclyffe's brother-in-law was commanding. I then went to the Anti-Tank Regiment, the Northumberland Hussars, and unfortunately just missed Dick Taylor who was commanding them.

Our next operation – Jupiter – started on 10 July when I led the Regiment from Norrey-en-Bessin across the River Odon near Verson to Chateau Fontaine. Here I was attached to B Squadron who proceeded to the top of the hill, commonly called Hill 112. It was a most unpleasant day as we were confined to our tanks for there was much shelling and sniping. There were some local advances and withdrawals by the infantry but nothing much could be done as there were some dug-in enemy tanks. The next day was equally bad – still never got out of our tanks except when I made a dive under a knocked-out Fife and Forfar Yeomanry tank with my shovel. David Callander led half of B Squadron into the wood to deal with some reported Tiger tanks. He had a most unpleasant and unfortunate time as two tanks, including his own, were knocked out by these previously reported dug-in tanks. He was quite admirable organizing everything from another tank after his own had been knocked out and then withdrew them without any further loss. I entered in my diary on the day: 'He did bloody well during the whole of this little battle and I reckon he ought to get an MC.' I am glad to say he got one. This was the third tank he had brewed up from under him, Azizia and Salerno being the other times.

The Regiment suffered a great blow at this place when a shell landed in C Squadron and killed Peter Paget. It was a great loss and Michael Williams took over the Squadron.

I was very glad the next day being allowed to go back to A Echelon to get something done to my tank for I had been 48 hours without a hot drink or meal, or a wash, and was dead beat – I had quite a bruise on my forehead as a result of continually dropping off to sleep and hitting my head on the turret! David had been burnt about the face the previous day so he was there as well and we had a pleasant day. We put some wild flowers on Peter's grave which was quite near and after a jolly good evening meal we sat and talked of old times over our whisky and cigars.

The next day I led the Regiment back over the river to an orchard near Byude Farm which was supposed to be a 'rest area'. The whole day we were subjected to stonks and several people became casualties including Sgt McMeekin. The following day we moved again to a proper 'rest area'. We left at first light and as we pulled off John Gunn and I noticed John Althorp's tarpaulin was still down and he had overslept! But he acted well and, when asked on the air if he was alright, replied that he was coming along in the right position – while he hurriedly packed up his kit!

We were here for eight days which was a nice rest for everyone except C Squadron who had to go back across the river to help some infantry. Rupert Milburn left us here to go to the Staff College and John Gunn went as 2i/c of B Squadron which meant that I took over Recce Troop. Early on the morning of 17 July RSM Anderton and Sgt March were both killed by a shell landing in their slit trench while asleep – very sad indeed. We all went to their funeral that morning and TQMS Milligan became RSM. In the evening two bombs fell in our area – one of them thirty yards away from my tank. We were luckily in a hole on the opposite side so only got covered in dust, although the tank got a large dent in the turret. We got our first bread ration and proper NAAFI issue of beer and chocolate since leaving England which cheered every-one up. There was an old partridge which used to sit and squawk near my tank at night, making all thoughts of war vanish.

We had all been expecting to help the attack in the area of Hill 112 again but on 20 July I was suddenly sent on a Recce with Brigadier Mike across the Orne as that became our destination. We started off in a heatwave when suddenly it clouded over and a solid sheet of water descended from the heavens. Literally, I've never known such rain in all my life – in Scotland, the tropics, Italy, anywhere. Within five minutes the roads were eighteen inches deep; all traffic off the road was stuck. Luckily I had taken my old macintosh but even then I was soaked to the skin, frozen and miserable. All the infantry we passed were soaked as they started off the day in shirt sleeves and hadn't a coat or groundsheet for miles and my Dingo had about 3 inches of water in the bottom. We came home via Caen, very slowly as there was so much traffic on the roads. I saw Joe Pennycock, who had been a Sergeant Major in the Regiment, on the way – he was leading some vehicles of 11th Armoured Division.

We moved on 22 July to a pleasant grass field near Carpiquet village, on the Bayeux-Caen railway line. They were in the process of mending this line and the workers got transported by a jeep with train wheels on. We were driven nearly mad here every evening by brown beetles, like cockchafers, which appeared in their myriads and flew about not looking where they were going, getting tangled up in one's hair and hitting one's face. It was amusing to watch everyone in the field chasing round trying to get rid of them or hitting them with improvised swats.

One afternoon Mo and I went to the aerodrome to find positions in the event of a counter-attack. As we arrived we heard what sounded like a pack of foxhounds in full cry. This turned out to be an odd assortment of alsatians, labradors, collies etc. which were pulling their soldier-masters helter-skelter across the field, stopping occasionally to point. We discovered they were dogs specially trained to find buried mines. They would point at an anti-personnel mine and stand astride a teller mine, so I was told.

The week we spent in this pleasant grass field was very peaceful and I went on several trips in the Dingo either on map-reading, finding mobile baths or egg and butter-collecting. John A and I went to the Scots Guards one day to find my brother-in-law Willie Whitelaw and a friend of John's. They were well set up in a pleasant spot near Bayeux and we had a drink before returning.

On 29 July we moved across the River Orne via Caen, which must have been a lovely old city before it was so badly bombed and shelled. The cathedral is an excellent example of plain, massive and stately Norman architecture which was a comparison with the other big church – a large overdecorated baroque monstrosity. Luckily the latter had received the most damage. We eventually arrived at our destination – the village of Ifs – and came under command of 2nd Canadian Division. The first night we were there Colonel Tim and I went up to A Squadron and while standing outside the Dingo talking a stonk of Nebelwerfers landed around us. Tim was nearer the only trench and got in first, with myself on top, so my back was above ground. Luckily Tim was no fatter, otherwise the bit of shrapnel which grazed me would have gone deeper. I spent two days with the Canadians at Hubert-Folie and Bourguebus, which was pleasant as they were all very nice and gave one drink and good food like chicken. The Regimental code names for these two places were 'Brassey's Mistake' and 'Enough Porridge'!

Some miniature robot explosive tanks called 'Beetles' attacked the village of Verrières where C Squadron were. They blew up with a tremendous explosion which blew the hats off people who were anywhere near. It was in this area that an extraordinary thing happened to Ian Dudgeon's[1] tank. He was outside it talking to someone when it was hit. When he went over to it, he could see nothing wrong until they opened the breech of the big gun and there, rammed up against the point of the AP shell in the chamber, was the AP shot that had hit the tank. It had gone right down the gun barrel and came to rest against the other shot whose soft nose was quite corkscrewed. Luckily for his crew it was not loaded with HE.

On 1 August C Squadron did an unsuccessful attack on Tilly-la-Campagne with the Calgary Highlanders. They lost two tanks and the infantry were unable to get into the village. One of the tanks was driven by Trooper Doug Smith (64), twin brother of Arthur, my driver. He was wounded but not badly. That night we moved back through Caen to our old area at Carpiquet where we remained for two nights before a long march to the right flank of the British Sector near Vire.

---

1 Lieutenant I. Dudgeon, Troop Leader.

CHAPTER XXIII

Falaise

O n 3 August we got to a small place called La Butte, just south of Bayeux, where we remained for two days during which time I got a new tank. I went to visit B Echelon who were in a delightful bit of country where Sgt 'Charlie' Taylor (a keeper's son from Aberdeenshire) told me he had seen many pheasants and rabbits. We then moved on by a very dusty tank track which by-passed Caumont and St Martin des Besaces and finished up in a pleasant bit of 'Bocage' country near Mont Bertrand. This 'Bocage' country consists of small grass fields surrounded by banks with thick hedges on top, the whole gently rolling, like parts of Northamptonshire. We were all made to dig trenches for we expected to be there for a few days but after losing a lot of weight digging we got a message to the effect that we were to move at 6 a.m. the next morning.

The move that morning was very pleasant going alongside a trout stream for a bit of the way with the harvest being cut. We stopped by a small farm for an hour or two where we had a brew. From then onwards there was a continual flap with 'rockets' flying. After a 'rocket' for being late in starting, we got to the village of Montisanger, about two and a half miles from Vire and while recceing the forward area in the Dingo, I lost my map and all my codes. Who should find them but the Colonel himself – another 'rocket'!

The first two days here were spent observing the enemy across a wide valley. On 9 August I went as LO to 2 KSLI with B Squadron who were to occupy the feature at Burcy. Luckily the enemy had withdrawn overnight so there was no opposition and the infantry and tanks drove into their positions. The only shots fired were by two riflemen who tripped up over their rifles which went off; and Sgt Thomson's tank set off a mine which broke the track. C Squadron had relieved the Fife and Forfar Yeomanry in the next village and I did a patrol on foot over towards them. Then after B Squadron had been relieved by 5th Guards Armoured Brigade, I led them back to RHQ by a very badly-marked tank track in inky blackness. I thought I was lost once but after crawling around on foot I picked up the track again. At one o'clock in the morning, while trying to guide the tanks through a very narrow sunken lane, Frank appeared to tell us to stop there the night, much to our relief.

On 11 August A Squadron supported an attack by 185 Brigade in which John Dawes's[1] tank was hit by a bazooka, at point-blank range, without doing any damage.

On 'The Twelfth' we went back from the area to Évrecy. It was a perfect day to be on the hill but there we were in our tanks going along a dusty track getting covered in this white powder. We soon met the tank transporters and while the Shermans loaded up we snatched a brew, for we went on our tracks by the main road via Beny Bocage and Villers Bocage to an area just short of Évrecy, the village which had been our objective in many unsuccessful actions during the previous two months.

We were here for Sunday morning and Padre Mac held a service in the orchard. That afternoon we crossed the Orne at Amaye and lea-guered in a field at Mutrecy. Having expected a long lie-in, we were woken early and were away by first light through the Forêt de Cinglais. After a brew near Fresnay-le-Vieux we moved on to Acqueville for the night. The next day we moved via Angoville to Pierrefitte-en-Cinglais.

On 16 August the Regiment supported 1 HLI of 71 Brigade in their advance to Martigny. During the morning I went around various neigh-bouring units in the area of Pierrefitte and the River Orne. This country was very attractive: deep gorges, large woods, pastureland, all looking and smelling fresh after the previous night's rain. The advance to Mar-tigny was practically unopposed and the Regiment leaguered there the night. The next day was spent in the same area and the expected move to the northern side of the Falaise Gap was put off a day. I did a recce round Falaise and got a good view of the country, but no enemy.

After breakfast we moved off, bound for the northern edge of the famous 'Falaise Gap'. We were to have had reveille at a quarter past five, so when I woke up at six-fifteen I got into a terrible flap and rushed round waking everyone up, thinking they had overslept,

---

1 Lieutenant J.S. Dawes, Troop Leader.

only to be told that reveille had been put back to six-thirty! The main Argentan–Falaise road was our centre line with CLY on our right. C Squadron led and soon got to a ridge which overlooked the only main road open to the retreating Hun. They took up positions on the left and A Squadron came up on the right. I took two sections to cover the wooded country between ourselves and the CLY. It was difficult going through the wood and I was later sent as LO to the CLY which was a nuisance as it tied me down to their RHQ and to make matters worse my wireless and Colonel Bill Rankin's, their CO, jammed each other when either spoke!

There appeared to be no organized resistance at this place although there were the odd enemy tank and gun, well hidden, which did damage. Peter Borwick, Ian Dudgeon and Gordon Edmiston[1] were all wounded and had to be evacuated. As Peter was taken back to the RAP on his Dingo Frank was heard to shout at him: 'Oh I say, Pete, have you got your chalumpjee?'[2] As Peter said afterwards, he didn't care a hang whether he had or not, he was feeling so miserable. There were several other rank casualties as well. It was estimated that about 150 vehicles of all sorts were knocked out by C Squadron during the day and 350 prisoners taken. On the following day A Squadron returned to their positions and caused considerable casualties to the enemy in both men and vehicles. The area where RHQ and Recce were was littered with abandoned and knocked-out vehicles. In the RHQ field a carthorse had been killed and its mate would not move away from it; it just stood with its head hanging over its dead friend looking very depressed. Even when we got the bulldozer to bury the dead one, it continued to stand over its grave.

That evening we moved back to an area just south of Falaise where we remained for two wet days. The Poles and Canadians in the meantime had closed the 'Gap' and everything seemed ready for the next pursuit.

On 22 August the Regiment moved to a concentration area just south of Trun. This was in a pleasant cornfield near the village of Tournay-sur-Dives whose church clock peacefully chimed the hours whilst all round was massed carnage of men, horses and vehicles, both motor and

---

1 Lieutenant G. Edmiston, Troop Leader.
2 Indian expression for washing kit.

Greys being remounted

horse-drawn. That afternoon I, like most of the officers, went off for a 'swan' to try and pick up a staff car or some other loot. It was all an amazing scene, these remains of a beaten army. When one did find an area clear of all this, it was very attractive. The following day I went out again beyond Trun, on the high ground. I visited a cheese farm where they were making a local form of Camembert. I saw it in all its stages, one of which was cutting a long twenty-yard strip of cheese into three-inch square blocks. Coming back through Trun I noticed a small street called Vennel de L'Église which was the same word as the Scots 'Vennel'. In the afternoon we collected a lot of stray horses and went out riding round the farms collecting butter. I felt pretty stiff even after a short ride! Shortly afterwards 'Greys' cigarettes issued an advertisement showing a very nice oil painting of our tanks here with the soldiers riding these loose horses bareback. It was probably painted from an article in *The Times* headed 'When the Greys were "re-mounted" at Falaise'.

> In the closing of the Falaise bag the regiment accounted for 400 German casualties and 500 enemy vehicles. It was here, too, that for a brief space the Scots Greys were "remounted". This part of France is famed for its breeding stock, and many fine horses were roaming loose, some with wounds from shell-splinter. The Greys were able to save many of them, and while resting the troopers gladly exchanged their Shermans for a hunter or cart horse.

We went to bed that night in pelting rain, having been told we were moving the next day at half-past nine to follow up the enemy in their retreat across France.

CHAPTER XXIV

Across France

On 24 August we started off from Trun to follow up the enemy, which we did without respite the whole way across France and into Belgium.

Progress on this day was very slow as all the small roads had traffic jams of Poles, Canadians or British. We eventually finished up for the night in a meadow by a stream near Aubri-le-Panthou having tried many different routes, each one being blocked. Poor Frank got badly bitten on the face by a wasp, both his eyes swelled up and he was like that for a day or two. The country round here was very hilly with many trees and small old farmhouses and chateaux dotted about.

The following day was one of the pleasantest spent during the War for we covered some sixty miles following the enemy who were many miles away. We were fêted in every town and village as liberators which is always most exhilarating especially when there is champagne as well. Shortly after starting off we passed through the grounds of a very nice chateau which had all its park railings painted white. Our route then lay through Mardilli, Chaumont, Le Sap André, St Nicholas des Laitiers, Le Ferte Fresnil, Glos La Ferrière to the River Risle where we were stopped opposite La Vieille Lyre by a blown bridge. In each of the villages we were given eggs, wine, fruit, flowers and kisses and were welcomed with open arms. Members of the FFI (French Resistance Movement), armed with every sort of weapon, also welcomed us. The only sign of war that day was a road block, booby-trapped with Teller mines which we left alone and found another route. We stopped at the river for about an hour as we were told not to cross, although two of my tanks had found fords and got over. We then received orders to come back to the Regiment at La Barre-en-Ouche and proceed to a small bridge in the next Brigade area near Ajou. We finished up for the night in an open cornfield outside Tilleul-Dame-Agnes.

The following day, as a precaution, I had to send out some patrols and spent the first part of the morning looking for John Althorp whom

I eventually found miles from where he said he was. I went through one small village which was flat from bombing; I suppose a convoy had been caught in it or it had been some HQ. Luckily at midday my patrols were recalled so in the afternoon John Briggs and I went on an egg-hunt; we managed to get some as well as tomatoes and butter. On Sunday morning the Padre never turned up for a church service so we all went out to play 'Partridge Polo'. There were endless acres of stubble round this place and we would drive about in jeeps till we put up a covey which usually scattered. Then we picked on a certain bird and followed it up till it got rather exhausted and would hide on the ground instead of getting up. If we could see it crouching we would drive past it and take a swipe with a stick. Sometimes we had a shot at one flying. Needless to say we never got one like this, although John Gunn fired at one on the ground with a pistol and found one dead and two winged with one shot. We got some more cream that night and climbed the church tower from where we had an excellent view.

We moved on again on 28 August to near Gaillon, just short of the Seine. It was a pleasant trip via Claville, Houetteville, Cailly and Ailly. Denis and I went for a walk and got a basket full of mushrooms which we had for breakfast the following day, which was very wet. It was a case of move, no move, move, no move etc. all day till four in the afternoon when we eventually did move. By that time we were all wet and miserable. The move, although only twelve miles, took eight hours and we eventually got across the Seine by a Bailey bridge at Ande and stopped the night at Le Mesnil Ande with a clear sky. The main road we went along followed the top of the steep bank above the river and we got a magnificent view both up and down.

Our orders for 30 August were to follow the Brigade in reserve up the main road to Gournay for the enemy were in full retreat. We left the Seine valley at Les Andelys which was an attractive old town with its ruined castle perched on an overlooking hill. There was a hotel looking like an old English coaching inn with a notice hanging outside saying 'English is spoken here'; I wondered if this notice had been there during the whole of the occupation or if it was put up to welcome us by the proprietor who was very pleased to see us. We climbed up onto the high ground just beyond this place and followed the main road to Morgny where we branched off to the left in order to enter Gournay by the Rouen road. Several enemy vehicles were reported by Sgt Cameron who eventually knocked out an armoured car, a Volkswagen and a motorcycle with his Stuart tank. Gournay was reached without further opposition and the Regiment was directed up the road leading to the north. A short way along this road a vehicle was spotted by C Squadron who thought it was an armoured car and engaged it with HE. Their shooting must have been accurate for on getting closer it turned out to be a Panther tank whose crew had been forced to abandon it and it was recovered later. We came across an airman who had been brought down some months previously and had been living with a French family. When he came back with us he seemed indeed sorry to go and there were some tender farewells with the daughter of the house. Reports of the large-scale retreat which came in frequently both from civilians and from Brigade put everyone in good spirits that evening, and the next morning we were up early and allowed to brew up before first light, as we did once or twice in the desert when the enemy were in rout.

We started off up the main road to Menerval then across to Grumesnil where some enemy infantry were seen in a field away to the right. I had Recce Troop in front with RHQ so I took mine and Cpl Randall's sections across to sort them out. We had a good hunt after them, over fields, ditches and hedges as they started to run away. However, a few bursts from our Brownings soon brought them to a halt and we got about thirty prisoners. We found their officer with an Iron Cross lying dead having been killed by one of our few shots. While this was going on A Squadron had run into some trouble at Canny and had lost two tanks, some of the crews being killed. After this delay I took one section and went ahead with B Squadron and we soon came upon some odd groups of enemy in a large wood near Courcelles. With the help of a section of C Company of the 60th they were cleared out. Then, owing to mines, we cut across country to Monceaux L'Arbbaye and along the main road to Broquiers. Here we found a mass of German horsed transport and infantry; some started to run away; others collected their arms and took up positions. We took a few prisoners, but on the arrival of B Squadrons's heavy tanks they all gave themselves up. There was a very highly-disciplined Nazi Sergeant Major among them who was very strict and would not allow any of them to give away information; however, one of the prisoners was a very amusing Alsatian who was only too willing to talk and kept pulling the Sergeant Major's leg and laughing at him, much to his rage. Off we went again well ahead of the heavy squadrons for we went much faster in our small tanks, and passed through the edge of Sarcus where we captured more prisoners and horsed transport. The crossroads at St Clair produced yet more; there I turned right and about half a mile away there was a large group of soldiers all dressed in different uniforms. I approached them and found sixteen American, Canadian and British ex-prisoners marching their one-time German guards towards us. By this time the others had caught us up and we stopped at Marlers where we received orders to proceed to the River Somme during the night. That set everyone flapping; however, it was cancelled soon afterwards and we had a decent night. Just as it was getting dark, RSM Milligan who was commanding A1 Echelon heard a lot of horses and carts trundling into the village he was in. He sent a patrol out to see what it was and they returned with eighty prisoners and a lot of horsed transport.

We started off early on 1 September. I followed B Squadron to start with but as there was no opposition my section took up the lead and we went by Bettenbos, Thieulloy L'Abbaye, Gouy L'Hopital to Camps-L'Amienois where Cpl Randall's tank broke down. However he was quite useful there looking after the prisoners and horsed transport which we took at nearly every village. The area between here and Molliens-Vidame held a few enemy who showed some fight until the arrival of C Squadron Shermans. Our route then lay across an open bit of country through Fayel and Montagne (where an old lady produced an excellent cup of tea) to Le Quesnoy-sur-Airaines. Here I had orders to recce a crossing of the small river Airaines between Bettencourt and Longpré where it flowed into the Somme. There were two bridges marked on the map at Bettencourt which turned out to be wooden. I got out of my tank to look at them when a mass of horsed transport appeared in the village the other side of the river. I shouted at Sgt Gargaro and Cpl Read who were still in their tanks to get across the bridge which appeared fairly strong. By the time we got into the village many must have escaped; however we captured several guns, transport and prisoners. In Longpré we were met by a well organized Maquis section who gave us information about the enemy.

We were now on the Somme and I was told to see if the bridge at Long were intact. This bridge had an approach of two miles of straight road and I confess I did not feel too happy going up it especially as I could see people running about the far end. We got to the bridge uneventfully and found that the river had split into three. We crossed the first two stone bridges and as we were rounding the corner to cross the last one which was wooden we were greeted by a hail of 20mm which struck the wall of the house beside us. B Squadron was close behind, so Sgt Dickinson brought his Sherman up and went round the corner to knock out the gun. We heard the 20mm gun fire and then over the air: 'William one Able, I'm blind, over.' We all thought he had been hit in the eyes, however, when Ian Readman,[1] his troop leader, asked him what had happened he replied 'William one Able, my periscope has been shattered.' So he wasn't much use and Ian Readman arrived in his tank and got a direct hit on the enemy gun as soon as he got into position. He reported that the bridge would not take tanks, so the Scissors bridge was brought up and laid among a fair amount of sniping. When this was done two B Squadron troops and myself and one section got across. While Tom Mahoney's[2] troop was crossing, Cpl Yule's tank slipped off the ramp and remained stuck so Tom's tank went up to tow it off but Haywood, who got out to fix the towrope, was killed by a sniper. The inhabitants of this village have since set up a memorial tablet to him on the wall above the spot where he fell. Tom himself then got out, fixed the rope and at the same time cut the wires leading to the demolition charges under the bridge. Sgt Edgar who was helping had a lucky escape – a sniper shot at him and the bullet went clean through the soft end of his nose. Tom's troop then got across and the OP from 6 Field Regiment followed, but his tank also slipped off and was hanging right over the bridge. It was obvious that this one could not be towed off and was blocking the bridge so he was given 'Abandon Ship' and the tank behind pushed tank and Scissors bridge into the river where it probably still is today. After that the REs declared the bridge too weak to take any more tanks so those that had got over went through the village and took up positions on the high ground

---

[1] Lieutenant I.R. Readman, Troop Leader.
[2] Lieutenant T.A. Mahoney, Troop Leader.

beyond. We were beside a cottage on the high ground beyond the village and the old woman from it came out with a basket of apples and a jug of fresh milk. There was spasmodic firing from a wooded island between two bits of the river but this was soon cleared by C Company at the expense of two casualties. B Squadron and my little party leaguered in the main street just across the bridge protected by C Company. A lot of houses were on fire and the village's very antedeluvian fire-cart came out to try and put the fires out. Two old men pumped a large double-handed pump all to no avail, for the water trickled out of the leaks. We were very glad that some of the houses were still burning for, when we came in at 10 p.m. in the dark, we were able to put our brew cans on one and soon had a hot cup of tea. We slept that night in the tanks for there were enemy round about at quite close range.

There was great indecision next day as to what we were to do. First we were told to come back across the river, then to stay over for a few hours and eventually we were told to remain till the morrow. I went back to the position I was in the night before and Cpl Randall kept watch at the western entrance to the village where he was attacked by infantry and 20mm guns. C Company were brought in and drove off this attack. I was told to do a sweep round the hillside to the west where the infantry were, so with Cpl Donnan we careered across this bit of ground directed by Duggie Stewart over the wireless who was on the hillside three miles away on the other side of the Somme. Our sweep brought us onto the road at Longest about a mile west of Long. We had to charge through the Manse garden to get to the road and sent the gate post spinning. We captured a Pole and destroyed a 20mm gun. When we got back to Long we spent the whole afternoon in the village, not on patrol, so we were able to have a good clean-up. There was an attractive small chateau overlooking the river which we explored. In the evening as it started to pelt I was told to go over to Ailly le Haut Clocher two miles away to contact CLY who were there. I took Sgt Gargaro's section and proceeded carefully across for lately some 88s had been firing from that area. However, we got over with no eventualities and spent a few hours with the CLY. We returned as it was getting dark and Sgt Gargaro's tank disappeared into a shell hole of the 1914-18 war; it took us a bit of time getting it out so we didn't get back till near midnight, when we took our bedding into a house where we found a spring bed, which I slept on, a fireplace and plenty of wood.

When the situation cleared up at Long, I was asked if there was anyone who should be put up for a decoration. The troop had done very well but then I reckoned it was our normal duty and so did not put any names in. If only I had known that my name had gone forward for an MC, I should certainly have put up one or two others for they did just the same as I did and it was very embarrassing when my MC arrived. Cpl Donnan was one who should have had an MM, as much as myself an MC, but I am glad that he got one later after crossing the Rhine.

On 3 September, my little party and B Squadron went via Ailly to Flixecourt where we met the remainder of the Regiment who had crossed the river at Picquigny. Our orders from there were to get to St Pol without going on main roads and to avoid any enemy pockets. So I set off with the Recce Troop leading and went via Domart, Berneuil, Bernaville and Maizicourt where we were stopped and told to come back to Bernaville as some enemy had been reported to our front. In the meantime one of the other Squadrons had been sent off in the lead which we were very annoyed about as we reckoned it was almost our right to lead on such occasions; so we did not take long to turn round and come back. We then tried the road to Le Meillard but were again stopped there by reports of the enemy, so we went around by Boisbergues, Mézerolles, Basly, Beauvoir, Bonnières and so on to the main road up which we proceeded for a short distance before pulling into a field to leaguer just south of Frevent. At Basly, an old woman came out of her house and rushed up to RSM Milligan excitedly waving a Regimental cap badge. She told him that she had been given it in the last war by a boyfriend of hers in the Regiment who had been billeted near there. She had a good memory, for she remarked, 'Of course, you had horses then.'

Beauvoir must have contained a V2 site or other important place, for the country for a radius of a mile around was a mass of bomb holes – a literal 'blasted heath'. It was difficult finding a way for the tanks between the holes.

On 4 September I sent out three patrols to the west and north of St

Pol, with the Squadrons in the same area. I took over one of the positions after going round the others and the section I relieved went on to St Martin Église. Between there and Croix they shot up some infantry and took four prisoners. My position was just outside the village of Troisvaux, whose inhabitants looked after us right royally during the two hours we were there; they brought us three dozen eggs, a dozen apples, a dozen scones, a loaf of bread, a pound of butter and fresh meat, besides a mass of flowers. Then every half-hour or so they would bring us a tray of sandwiches, tea, sugar and an enormous pot of cream. We could hardly say that we did not live well in those days. They also appeared with the documents of an RAF crew who had been killed when their bomber was shot down near the village. They had all been buried in the churchyard so I sent the documents on to RHQ.

At midday we all reassembled at RHQ where we spent the remainder of the day and in the evening we were told that 4th Armoured Brigade was to cross into Belgium and join 7th Armoured Division in the Ghent area.

CHAPTER XXV

Belgium

On 5 September we left St Pol and made for Belgium via Aubigny, Hersin, Vermelles, Carvin and Seglin and crossed the frontier at Toufflers. It was a slow journey through very pleasant rolling country until we reached the top of the escarpment at Hersin whence we had a horrible view of the French 'Black Country' covered in smoking lums and bings. The people grew nicer the nearer we got to Belgium and got more like Britons in looks and manners. We stopped for several hours at the frontier as our orders had been changed for there was a strong enemy pocket on our original route and we had to go further to the south. The frontier there was only a small six-inch ditch across the open fields and a 'Douane-Tol' house and barrier on the road. After starting off again I led the Regiment through Estambourg to Éspierres where I saw, and stupidly ignored, a notice at a crossroads: '*Le pont est tombé*', later finding out to my cost that the bridge over the canal had been blown so everyone had to turn round and cut across to the main road leading north to Courtrai. Here we heard that there was enemy south of Courtrai in the village of Belleghem so A Squadron took up positions on the high ground each side of the main road overlooking Courtrai and Sgt Cameron's section went into Belleghem, capturing fifteen prisoners. I followed him a few minutes later and found the local Maquis very well organized with the village hall packed with German prisoners they had taken. The Maquis said that the members of their movement had risen against the Germans in Courtrai and were having a very tough time – 'Could you help them?' Although everyone was very keen to we could not leave our positions. I then went and visited their local HQ in a farm nearby where everything was well laid on: sentries on the gate, Ops room, CO's room, prisoners under guard, etc. They were very thrilled when my tank, small though it was, rumbled into the farmyard. As I got down I was presented with a huge bouquet of flowers and embraced for several minutes by the Maquis leader's wife. I then entered the Ops Room amid a lot of heel-clicking and saluting. I got a fair amount of information off them and returned to Belleghem, before coming back to leaguer at RHQ where I found out that my Dingo had broken down a few miles away with some of my kit, so that wasted another hour or so.

At 3 a.m. we were all aroused and told to get ready to move immediately. After we had all started up, I saw Colonel Tim and Richard laughing and telling everyone to stand down and go back to bed. The rear link had received a message 'Why haven't you moved yet?' and Richard very naturally thought we ought to have moved on somewhere so had got everyone ready while he found out where we were supposed to go to. What Brigade really meant was why hadn't we moved our frequency on the wireless which should have been done at midnight!

After we got up again I sent half the troop off to the high ground we were on the day before and left the remainder round a farm near St Genois. Sgt Cameron who had gone back to Belleghem found another 150 prisoners, so he organized a Maquis guard who marched them back to the PW cage. I went on up to join him and was asked in by the village Doctor for a delicious meal of eggs, bacon and tomato. In the afternoon, the enemy who were surrounded tried to break through to the south just to the east of our positions at Avelghem. B and C Squadrons were in position looking north-west and north from the high ground north of this place and A Squadron was passed through them towards Ooteghem where there appeared to be a large concentration of enemy infantry and horsed and motor transport. Although there was a tongue of enemy between ourselves and 44 RTR our tanks were not allowed to fire their big guns, as the latter regiment was only 2-3,000 yards away, but they fired over 4,000 rounds of Browning machine-gun, killed about thirty Germans, captured 150 and knocked out countless vehicles. Sgt Eastway's troop went right through the village which was packed with enemy transport from which he got prisoners to drive back to our lines thirteen lorries and several cars including a full Colonel Doctor in a very smart Mercedes. Cpl Bruce's tank was ditched on the way out and Tpr Mylie was killed when the enemy started to mortar the tank which was eventually set on fire. There was a considerable amount of sniping and Sgt Killin was unfortunately killed, one of the last of the A Squadron Sergeants of pre-mechanized days, and a great loss to the Regiment. For the night, B and C Squadrons guarded the northern and eastern entrances to Avelghem where RHQ and A Echelon were leaguered, while A Squadron remained guarding the southern exits from Ooteghem. It was an unpleasant night for no one quite knew where the enemy was; someone dropped their Sten gun which went off and we all thought an enemy patrol had come in; and then we had to wait till 2.30 a.m. for the petrol replenishment to arrive in pelting rain.

The morning of 7 September dawned most unpleasant – still raining hard, combined with many rumours. Some of us managed to get a cup of hot coffee from a café opposite the tanks before stand-to. Before B Squadron moved into position Andrew Mercer[1] was walking round the Squadron area and as he turned a corner in the street he came face to face with a German officer doing the same. Both were caught unawares without arms and turned tail and disappeared. As soon as his troop moved out of leaguer they were fired on by HE and hit. As he reversed he ran into another tank in his troop and got locked together. The remaining troop tank attempted to pass and got ditched. Tom Mahoney's tank also got ditched and Sgt Thomson's was knocked out. By this time two companies of enemy infantry were infiltrating through the B Squadron positions so Sgts Collins and Muirhead dismounted their Brownings and together with guns and crews of the ditched and knock-out tanks organized ground defence which delivered such heavy fire that the attack was temporarily broken up. There were two 88mm guns which still caused trouble to B Squadron and A Squadron on the left so I was told to take all members of RHQ, Recce and AI Echelon who were not engaged in any particular job and get positions in suitable houses overlooking the enemy; L/Cpl Kendall and North had gone off on their own to a house and with a Bren killed the crews of the two 88s. With RSM Milligan's help we organized a good position in a house on the edge of the town which had a good view of the enemy area. We had several Brens, Stens and rifles and did a lot of shooting which, although probably not causing many casualties, kept the enemy's heads down. We watched a very brave act when two members of the Maquis attempted to crawl through a turnip field out to a large farm occupied by the enemy. They got halfway when one was wounded in the arm and the other then had to help him back. The RSM was wounded by

---

1   Lieutenant A. Mercer, Troop Leader.

flying glass from enemy fire and had to be evacuated. We remained there about two hours, having had to send a runner back for more ammunition, until a platoon of C Company relieved us. In the afternoon an attack on the enemy was carried out by two companies of 9th Cameronians supported by C Squadron. They got to their objective after much MG and mortar fire, C Squadron losing two tanks in the attack. After this all Squadrons were told to withdraw as the enemy appeared to have quietened down. B and C Squadrons remained in Escanaffles. As attempts were being made to tow away some of the broken-down tanks, Sgt Crompton in one of the tanks guarding this operation noticed two lines of Germans twenty yards away in the dark. He fired and they hurriedly scattered, having evidently thought that all our tanks had gone. Many tanks were left out that night and next morning they were untouched which showed that the enemy had completely evacuated that area and were trying to escape from the net somewhere else.

Shortly after first light on 9 September B and C Squadrons rejoined the Regiment at Escanaffles having been relieved by 44 RTR. Then at eight o'clock we all moved to Lokeren via Oudenarde, Sottegem, Alost and Termonde. Before reaching Termonde, a Sapper was sent there to see if the bridge would take 28-ton Sherman tanks. He said it was alright, but nearly passed out when he arrived to see the last tank of the Brigade going over a very weak bridge which had some supports sawn away and, he reckoned, would only take five-ton. He had originally looked at the wrong bridge!

As Tiger tanks were reported on the north-east outskirts of Lokeren, the approach to this place was by a side road though Everslaar. Soon the whole Regiment had got into Lokeren with no opposition and took up positions covering the entrance over bridges to the town from the east, north and west. RHQ and A Echelon moved into the centre of the town and I had several sections out, chiefly contacting the 11th Hussars who had patrols in the vicinity. That night was spent peacefully and comfortably in abandoned shops, in spite of a few shells arriving nearby.

The next day the Regiment was ordered to occupy St Nicolas and clear the vicinity of enemy. Recce led the Regiment via Waesmunster to Belcele. Between these two places there were a lot of concrete and earth buildings on a hill in a wood which were presumed to be a V2 site. From Belcele, I led along the bypass when I thought it would be wiser to have a section in front of me in case we met up with some enemy. As Corporal Randall passed, a Gunner jeep and staff car came careering towards us saying that there was an enemy column the other side of the railway a few hundred yards ahead. Cpl Randall went forward cautiously and drew much small arms fire. Rory la Terrière's[1] troop came up to deal with it and one of his tanks was hit. It was suspected that this was only a small group of enemy trying to escape and that they would soon turn round and look for a new route, so I was sent round to the right with one of my sections via Klitterbosch to Zonneken which was at the east end of the bypass where we arrived only a few minutes after the enemy had left. However our journey was not wasted for we were given an enormous egg omelette each and a drink! By this time St Nicholas had been occupied and the vicinity reported clear. We returned via the bypass and then had to go and look for John Althorp who had gone on a recce to the south and whose wireless set had broken down. Having contacted him we proceeded to the leaguer area in an orchard where there was rather a muddle getting in as a guide was not put on the gate to the orchard and we overshot it and had to turn round in a very narrow lane in the dark.

The next day the Regiment occupied the country between St Nicolas and the Schelde just south of Calloo which was the eventual objective. We sat in Melsele for some time in the morning. I had a long chat to a dear old farmer, aged seventy, who was immaculately dressed in his Sunday best with flowing white moustache. Later on I visited my various patrols in the area of Zwyndrecht where there was a large embankment of some road under construction from which we got a good view of Calloo. In the evening the local Maquis, called 'The White Brigade' made an unsuccessful attack on Calloo and were badly shot up by a machine-gun which A Squadron engaged.

There was no activity next day and the Regiment concentrated in a field in front of the Château in Beveren Waes. At first light I sent out two patrols to the area just short of Calloo who reported nothing. The Polish Armoured Division arrived during the afternoon to take over

---

1 Lieutenant F.J.R. de Sales la Terrière, Troop Leader.

our positions and the Regiment started on its way back to an area near Mechlin where it was to have four days' rest. Our route was via St Nicholas, Lokeren, Wetteren and Wichelen, a small village on the river Escaut, where we spent a night. There was a hideous church in Wetteren with a tall spire which could be seen for miles, a marked contrast to a charming little brick and stone church at Calcken which must have been very old. There were tram-like trains running along the side of these roads and occasionally one would hear a 'toot' and on looking round, there would be a train trying to pass you. The next morning we completed the journey via Termonde, Willebroeck, Mechlin, to Heyst-op-den-Berg which was to be our home for the next five days. It was here that Smith 25 returned to me as driver. He had continued to drive Astra when I left RHQ in March, but he did not get on with John Parkin so I swapped him with my driver Robb, who had done me so well all through France. We passed 'Monty' on the way and arrived at lunchtime, when we had a visit from a 'Stop-me-and-buy-one'. Recce was in a field outside an old moated farmhouse with RHQ next door. The Officers' Mess lorry came up and we made ourselves comfortable. We had not been in this place for two hours before we were surrounded by children, some playing football with the men, some washing clothes, some washing up while others just stood and stared.

This rest we had was very pleasant for we had never slept in the same place for two nights running since leaving Normandy. The time was spent maintaining tanks, sleeping, going for walks, a Church Parade and a trip to Brussels, which practically everyone did. After polishing up my Sam Browne belt and tidying my service dress which had been packed since leaving Worthing, I went in with David Callander and several others. We travelled in state in a 15cwt truck and got there about midday. As soon as we got out, we were set upon by an old lady weeping with joy at speaking to Britons – Brussels had only been liberated a few days. We had been told of an excellent restaurant called the Savoy in the main boulevard and on our way there we found a place where we could get a drink. On entering we were told by two men it was a private club but would we be their guests? Naturally we accepted! We were surprised when Scotch whisky (at a price) and English gin (at a slightly less price) were produced. After thanking them in our best French, we made our way to the Savoy which turned out to be next door. Here we had a superb lunch of chicken, mushrooms, strawberries etc. which cost us £2 10s 0d. each so it was a pity we did not find a 'fairy Godmother' here – all the same it was worth paying that for such good food. We spent the afternoon going round the main shops in the Rue Neuve reviving ourselves on the way in the Gunthers of Brussels called Kiez. On a tram I met a lady who kindly asked me to dinner but as she lived outside Brussels I did not have the time so we had a huge dinner in the Savoy and got back to the Regiment at eleven – weary but contented after a few hours of civilization again.

On Sunday the 17th a mass of troop-carrying planes and gliders passed over us on their way to Nijmegen and Arnhem. It was a most impressive sight. The following day we left this place to be operational again on the canals near Bree. It was a big effort packing up after spreading ourselves for several days but we got away after an early lunch. I had to go ahead to recce the routes so went in Richard's jeep, driven by 'Jackie' Pert. Our route was via Aerschot, Montaigu, Diest, Spalbeek (where we crossed the Albert Canal) and Helchteren, and finishing up for the night at Meenween with the Squadrons in the villages around. It was here that we found a large market garden with many greenhouses of delicious grapes.

The next few days were spent in patrolling this area and watching the canal near Tongerloo and Opitter. The enemy had some infantry on our side of the river but they never showed any aggressiveness.

The Recce Troop was, as usual, hard at it most of the time as these patrols were their job and not the heavy tanks'. I did a lot of running about between sections and visited a Belgian Armoured Car Squadron in the neighbourhood whose Squadron Leader was very nice, having been wounded and taken prisoner in 1940 and then sent home as incurable. However, he was fit enough to escape to England where he trained with the rest of the Belgian Brigade for the liberation of their country. We started the RHQ Mess here which was pleasant and I used to supplement the rations with mushrooms and eggs. I came across a field which was white with the former and after picking three sandbags full the field was still white. I paid a visit to the Chateau at Gruitrode which was a pleasant example of a small moated manor. We were shown the interesting parts by a priest who was living there. It was built in 1534 (the date was on the gatehouse), ruined in the 1914–18 War and restored.

On 22 September when we arrived at our post a mile from Opitter, we got many civilian reports that the enemy had withdrawn across the canal so Cpl Randall and I entered Opitter and Solt to find them clear. The Burgomaster at Opitter had given us each an English-speaking guide and Randall went to the blown bridge at Tongerloo while I went to Solt. Here an old man, who looked very like Joe Dudgeon, came out of his house and gave us each an enormous plateful of fried eggs and pork which I started to eat with great gusto until Colonel Tim appeared. I expected he would be very annoyed but I got 'Joe Dudgeon' to bring him a similar plateful which delighted him and he leant against my tank eating it and other food that was produced.

Sgt Cameron, my Troop Sergeant, got very annoyed with Tpr Tom Laidlaw when they were observing on the canal for when he asked him to 'Chuck out the torch', Laidlaw, always obeying orders to the letter of the law, hurled the torch out which smashed into smithereens. 'But you did say "chuck it out"' was his argument!

A Squadron moved down to this place and took over from Recce Troop, but on the evening of the 24th the Regiment concentrated near Neerglabbeek preparatory to moving into Holland. While there Sgt Field and some Belgians came running up and told me there was a wild goose sitting in a field half a mile away – did I want to shoot it? Sgt Field produced a service rifle for me; I took aim and fired at this speck in the distance. It didn't get up so I presumed I had shot it. There was a rush of Belgians to it and they appeared back with a heron, shot through the neck – a good shot, but not the right sort of bird!

CHAPTER XXVI

Holland

On 26 September we moved into Holland via Bree, Kinroy (which surely should have been in Scotland, by its name), Stamproij and Weert to Nederweert where we took over positions on the Willems Vaart Canal, also known as the Bois le Duc Canal. RHQ and Recce were centred round a group of houses at Hesterstraat about a mile west of Nederweert and the Squadrons manned positions on the canal. The old farmer in whose fields and barns we lived was very kind and gave us all sorts of fresh food.

On 28 September Sgt Cameron, my troop Sergeant, who was in an OP at the cross canals, was sniped in the shoulder and died on the way back to the Regimental Aid Post (RAP). He had been an excellent and helpful Troop Sergeant and he was sadly missed by the whole Troop. He was buried that evening by Father Copay from Brigade in the field beside our tanks. The locals were very nice and brought lovely flowers. The next day John Perkins,[1] a new officer who had just arrived the day before, was killed at breakfast along with his crew (Tprs Hall and Jeffries). They were buried beside Sgt Cameron. After the war the inhabitants set up a large stone cross behind the graves with an inscription in Dutch 'Let us not forget the Royal Scots Greys'. When the central war cemetery was made in Nederweert, this stone cross was made centrepiece of the graveyard. The Regiment has always had a soft spot in its heart for Nederweert and its people, and were able to send the Band and the Pipes and Drums there in 1949 to beat retreat on their tour in Holland.

From one of our OPs we could see a ferry on the canal which was continually used by the enemy. We worked out a plan that, when we gave the codeword 'Baker Sixteen' over the air as the ferry was about to leave, the tank which was laid on this target fired at the opposite shore, where the shell's and the boat's arrival coincided!

---

1 Lieutenant J.A. Perkins, Troop Leader.

While we were there I climbed the church tower several times which made an admirable OP as it commanded such a large tract of enemy country. Once up and down was enough exercise for a week for there were over 200 steps. One felt very safe up there inspite of German shells hitting it for it was several feet thick in brick all round.

One day Brigade sent a Dutch lady to spy for us who soon became Richard Shelley's best girl! She was very pretty and although her full name was Der Jankrouwe L. E. Baronesse Van Hardenbroek Van Der Kleine Linde, she was soon known by shorter and more appropriate names. She did several patrols into enemy-held country and eventually left us by swimming the canal and making her way to Roermond, about fifteen miles away. Richard saw her again after the War.

Two days before leaving here I had to set up patrols on the canal running north as far as Someren. This was a pleasant break as we were away from the Regiment during the day and had our comfortable sheds and barns to return to at night. I liaised with a retired Dutch naval commander who lived on the canal and took a leading part in the local resistance movement as well as helping many Jews and other persecuted persons to escape from Germany. We spent two very pleasant days in these positions until 3 October when the Regiment was relieved by 4th Bn Grenadier Guards of the 6th Guards Brigade (Churchill tanks), and we made our way up to the 'Island' – that bit of land surrounded by two branches of the Rhine between Arnhem and Nijmegen.

As usual I was sent ahead to recce the route which went through Leende, Helmond, Gemert, Uden to a large fir wood south of Grave. The weather was vile – hail, rain and sleet most of the day and I was frozen in my Dingo but managed to get a cup of coffee at a few places. It cleared up in the evening and was very pleasant so I strolled over to A Squadron and helped out 'Chas' with his whisky – pure white stuff! – which he got regularly from home in tin containers marked 'medicine'. The following day we moved on again over the Maas at Grave and then the Waal at Nijmegen. Both these bridges had been captured by the Airborne troops and were intact. It was unfortunate that they hadn't managed to hang on to the Arnhem bridge as well.

For two weeks the Regiment remained on the 'Island' – not so much acting in an armoured role as being there to keep up the morale of the infantry. All movement by forward Squadrons had to be done under cover of darkness for they were under observation from the high ground at Arnhem. Both the infantry and conditions were not unlike those at Salerno after landing.

RHQ and Recce lived together the whole time – the latter only being used in a liaison role. Our first area was at Oosterhout which we took over from the 13th/18th Hussars. We ate in a large barn surrounded by animals and in the middle of a meal one day, the farm dog produced puppies under the sideboard! From this place we went to a very nice spot near Herveld beside a burned-out farm under the bund which ran parallel to the Waal and about a hundred yards from it. We didn't stay there more than a few days for we were heavily shelled one morning. I was watching the shelling at a safe distance when I was hit on the head by a spent bit of shrapnel. I thought it was a chestnut falling off a tree until I found the piece at my feet. From here we moved to a frightful farm near Valburg surrounded by very heavy guns which fired all night. We ate in the house but slept in the mud outside. Hugh composed an appropriate poem about this awful place where RHQ had parked itself, which began something like this:

I cannot understand why RHQ
Never behaves like me and you . . .

When we were in the area beside the river, Ted Rob and I used to go out shooting some evenings with a rifle and pistol hoping to get a roosting pigeon which, needless to say, we never did; one night we went down to the river and sat on the side hoping a duck might conveniently settle near enough to have a crack. There were plenty flighting up and down but none came near. When we were there we heard a wireless blaring in the distance so we went to investigate and found it was Colonel Tim's jeep on the bund with the wireless full on so that he could hear what was going on while he stalked duck with his sniper's rifle which he had just procured from the 60th!

We were under 101st US Airborne Division during our stay in this area and I spent four days at their HQ as LO. It was quite pleasant as the Yanks were very nice and gave us good food. Everyone in the headquarters used to queue up for their food at the cookhouse except the General whose ADC collected his. Many of us made friends and money with the Americans for they would give the equivalent of £10 for a German Luger pistol of which we had any amount!

Most tanks got well stocked with jam and sugar for there were many factories on the Island. One day Colonel Tim was at Divisional HQ and on his way back he heard a conversation on the air between Frank at RHQ and Hugh at B Squadron all about jam and marmalade and which it ought to be. The Colonel thought they were two code names for some counter-attack and came rushing back until he convinced himself they were talking about food; he then blew up on the wireless and gave them a terrific rocket for wasting time on the air!

There was only one fatal casualty here and that was Sergeant Beatson who was killed by shrapnel when in the turret of his tank – an unfortunate way for such an excellent young tank commander to be killed.

On 18 October we moved out of the Island having been relieved by the 13th/18th and came under 4th Armoured Brigade again. Our route was via Nijmegen, Grave, St Oedenrode, Eindhoven, Bladel to Lage Mierde where RHQ established itself in a nice group of farmhouses. As soon as we arrived I was sent off to A Squadron as second-in-command until Chas returned from his forty-eight hours' leave in Brussels. This was great fun as they were in Hilvarenbeek, a village some six miles in front of RHQ, together with a squadron of the Royal Dragoons. I was only there for twenty-four hours but returned again when Duggie had to go off for an interview so I did second-in-command to Chas for a day. Luckily I didn't go there a day earlier for a German patrol had got right up to an A Squadron troop and fired bazookas at them without doing any damage, except causing a flap.

We were fairly comfortable with RHQ and slept the first two nights in the farm kitchen which we shared with the old farmer who slept in an old built-in box bed. We decided to move from here as the womenfolk sat up so late in the kitchen it meant we had to undress in the scullery and then quickly nip back and jump into bed. We then pitched the mess tent which three of us shared.

I lost one of my tanks here in a most annoying way. Cpl Read was bringing his back from workshops and was straddled by our own Spitfires on the way. The tank brewed up and he and Barker were slightly wounded – Bourne, the driver, luckily getting away with it.

I did one or two patrols from this area. We either went to a place where the enemy had been reported the previous day or else the enemy were reported at the place where *we* had been the previous day. The country was all thick woods and the enemy appeared to send roving patrols through them which made it hard for us to catch up with them. Their patrols sometimes went into Esbeek, B Squadron's village, so they laid some trip flares at the entrance and turned out one night when one was set off but it turned out to be a dog.

On 23 October Ted Acres completed three years commissioned service and became a Captain QM. Tony Bonham, with the help of his Dutch landlady, decorated Ted's room and sewed up his pyjama legs. On arrival back at a late hour after replenishment he didn't think the latter a bit funny!

The day before we moved from there John, Cpls Donnan and Kelly and I went on a recce of our next route and came back through the woods hoping we might shoot some game. We saw several pheasants and hares and a few roe deer but never got a shot. That evening Ted and I wandered round the woods at RHQ with a gun and got two pheasants, one of which was roosting!

On 26 October we started off for the operation to capture Tilburg and advance to Breda, and got as far as Straat Akkers for that night. On the way a skein of over a hundred greylag flew over, much to everyone's excitement. We were allowed to go into billets and John A, Ted R and myself got an excellent farmhouse in which we sat round the fire that evening reading with a drink and the wireless going. Our orders the next day were to cut the road leading west from Tilburg and to deny it to the enemy evacuating this place. However, owing to demolitions we only got, via Poppel, to Goirle just south of Tilburg. We started off at first light the next day and by-passed the centre of Tilburg which had already fallen. No opposition was encountered until reaching the road junction leading to Reijen where enemy infantry were seen. The Squadrons were then told to clear Reijen while C Squadron of the Royals protected the left flank and Recce Troop the right. The south of the village was easily occupied but enemy infantry were encountered to the west and north. As it was getting dark so the Squadrons withdrew to a leaguer area at the southern end of the village for the night. During the day I had several sections out between Reijen and Tilburg. From one of them 7th Armoured Division could be seen advancing on the other side of the Wilhelmina canal. Early the next morning while two troops of A Squadron were brewing up, a salvo of mortars landed amongst them killing SSM Robertson and Tpr Hunter, mortally wounding Rory de Sales la Terrière and wounding eleven others. This was a great blow to the Regiment as well as to A Squadron, who were relieved by C Squadron as a result.

The remainder of 4th Armoured Brigade were withdrawn back to Weert and Colonel Tim was left in command of Readforce consisting of ourselves, 2 KRRC, Royal Netherlands Bde, G Battery 4 RHA and a troop of REs. It appeared that the enemy had evacuated Reijen leaving many booby traps and some snipers. I went to the 60th Battalion HQ as LO for the night and had a good dinner with them; according to custom, the prisoners captured during the day were marched in by the RSM and interrogated by their CO, Colonel Robin Hastings. I got back to RHQ the next morning to find that we were moving shortly to rejoin the Brigade in the Kinroy area. We left about midday and had a miserable cold and wet journey via Goirle, Poppel, Aerendonck, Eindhoven, Valkenswaard, Leende, Weert and Kinroy where we arrived in pitch dark at nine to find nothing arranged or laid on. The last part of the journey was very difficult in the inky blackness. We nearly got lost in Weert, and, at a level crossing near Maarheeze, SSM Shaw turned too soon in his Dingo and drove for some distance down a railway line before realizing it. Tony Bonham was taking B Echelon to Opitter and tried to go via a blown bridge but had to turn the whole Echelon round in the dark in a narrow road. Eventually, after a two-hour conference I got to bed after midnight exhausted.

We remained in this area for a fortnight but after two days moved to a very nice farm which was approached by half a mile of knee-deep mud and surrounded by the same; that was its big drawback. The farmhouse was large and modern, the farmer being a scruffy old man who, the story goes, heavily insured his old farm, burnt it down and built this one on the proceeds. He had a large, attractive daughter called Bertha – hence Bertha's Farm, as we named it. RHQ was based on this house and I had a small cottage, a room in which I shared with Ted Rob. The owners were very nice and supplied us with pork, vegetables, and other fresh food. My troop used to sit round the fire in the evenings gossiping with the family. I went back there one day after the War and they were overjoyed at seeing someone from the Regiment. I messed with RHQ in the farmhouse where we had the large sitting room which was very comfortable. There was a bath with a geyser where we all had our first bath since leaving Worthing at the beginning of June!

We had one or two dinner parties here. One evening Frank had asked some high-ranking friend and after dinner produced, with great éclat, a bottle of 'port' he had got in Brussels. He was a bit perturbed when he drew the cork, which had the name of some brandy stamped on it, and even more perturbed when he tasted it to find it was a horrible, sweet, sickly Marsala! Hugh and I dined at Rear Army HQ with Matthew Arthur and John Prideaux one day, who were in a very nice Schloss at Sonnis. Another evening I went over to dine at C Squadron with David Callander who had heard the sad news of his brother Archie being killed.

We had an area here which we were responsible for under 53rd Welsh Division. The Dutch-Belgium border ran through this bit and when we were recceing the small tracks, one passed back and forward across the frontier which was only marked by a five-foot metal obelisk with the Royal Arms of the Netherlands on one side and those of Belgium on the other with a date and obelisk number on it. I visited a squadron of 53 Recce who were cooperating with us and was very surprised when the Squadron Leader thought I was some full Colonel he was expecting and treated me as such; I had quite a time making him believe I wasn't! There were some attractive little villages beside the River Meuse where we had patrols occasionally – Thorn, Neeritter and Ittervoort being the nicest. When there were no patrols or recces to be done, parties were sent to Bree for baths and a cinema, and a certain number allowed forty-eight hours' leave in Helmond or Brussels.

The town of Maeseyk was only two or three miles away and I used to go there quite often. It was on the river, the other side of which was enemy-held so not many troops had been in. I found the shops full of good stuff and I invested in a thermos, cutlery, food, a pair of clogs which I used to wear in the mud, and many other useful things. It had a most attractive square, very much like Kelso and I realized why H. V. Morton likened this border Burgh to a continental town. All the children of the town were thrilled at seeing soldiers and when a lot clustered round the Dingo I told them I was 'Monty'. They could not quite make it out but the next time I was in, they ran after me laughing and shouting 'Here's Monty!' We often used to go out with a gun round this place where there was some decent country and occasionally got a partridge, pigeon or hare which made a welcome addition to the army rations, which, as a matter of fact, were not bad, as sometimes we were given captured German army rations, some articles of which were excellent such as their Ryvita-type biscuit call '*Knäckebrot*', frozen peas and beans etc.

I was sent off one day to some HQ at Bourg Leopold to fix up a range a short distance behind us. I dealt with a very 'Poona' Major who assured me he would send a 'fast-running Coolie' – a DR – with a reply. This range was used a lot and a demonstration was given by C Squadron one night showing direction-finding by firing tracer in the required direction from behind and over the heads of the leading troops. The results were highly successful. Another useful demonstration was staged by B Squadron and Recce Troop showing what size ditches could be crossed by different tanks and the difference the various tracks made in soft going. Instead of going to the ranges, Mo Williams decided to 'Fire-in' one of his new Firefly 17-pounder guns by shooting into enemy country, so he parked the tank outside a cottage near Ophoven. He and I, from beside the cottage, watched the tank commander laying the gun and when it fired every tile came off the roof, and all the windows blew *out*, luckily, as the family had their noses glued to the windows and would have been badly cut had they blown *in*. We just got out of the way of the tiles in time. Mo was very embarrassed and did not know what to do so we jumped into our vehicles and drove away!

My old tank, Glensax, which had brought me safely the whole way from Worthing had to go away for a new engine so I took one of the new Stuarts which had the self-change Cadillac gearbox. This was a good excuse for Smith, my driver, and I to go for a swan in it to practice driving with this patent gearbox.

The Python scheme – the posting home of those with three years service abroad – was published here and it was obvious that the Regiment would be hit very badly by losing some 250 old soldiers including virtually all senior ranks. The Colonel went to Army HQ about it and proposed that the Regiment as a whole should go home so as not to break up the present smooth-running organization. An alternative to this was: 'Could the majority of those affected take a month's leave and return to the Regiment, as they had volunteered to do that?' It turned out eventually that the latter alternative would be allowed, hence the commencement of LILOP – Leave in lieu of Python. There was a lot of speculation waiting for the final decision and many cartoons and jokes were made about Python.

On 8 November we were told to move to a new area south-west of Weert so Frank and I went to recce it. It was quite a nice place and the whole Regiment could get under cover in two villages. From then until we did actually move on the 14th, there were the twice-daily orders to move, don't move, move, don't move. In the end we did not move to this place at all but went to Stamproij where we concentrated for the forthcoming operation 'Mallard' whose objective was to clear the enemy from all the country west of the Meuse. By this time winter was upon us and we had our first snowfall. It was cold and generally wet so everyone hoped for a speedy operation.

We spent two days in the concentration area while the preliminary attacks were made and a bridge built across the Wessem Canal. The house we were billeted in was full of old men and women, young boys and girls and children and I had a frightful row with them one evening when I asked them to leave the room while we had a conference. They did so in the end very grudgingly but afterwards we became friends again and finished up playing 'rummy' with them. We eventually got across the canal on the 16th after interminable delays but luckily with no fighting as the enemy had withdrawn. The first night we slept under the stars in a temperature below freezing. On the way to the canal I had met Peter Bowlby in the Fife and Forfar Squadron. He was a young cousin of Frank's and I used to know him before the War in Peeblesshire – a far cry from the Wessem canal. The next day the Regiment moved into billets west of Baexem leaving B Squadron still forward. I had a nice house for Recce and shared a sitting room and bedroom with Ted again. The Burgomaster of Roermond was living there, having hidden from the Germans for three years. He spoke French and I stupidly said that I did, so he spent the whole time gabbling French which naturally we could not understand. Laidlaw caused a scare one evening when he told us one of the men living there was a German, so we went in to talk to them all and he turned out to be a harmless Dutchman. We moved on the 29th to prepare for the final push to the river. Ted and I were annoyed about this as our old farmer had asked us to go shooting with him that day.

We moved via Baexem, Hejhuizen, Roggel, Beringe, Panningen, to Vosberg where we spent the night in a farm which we managed to get after a fight over it with an infantry platoon and a gunner troop. In one of the rooms the dead owner lay on his bed as he had been killed by a shell. Some gunner who arrived late at night walked into his room, shone his torch onto the corpse and nearly died of fright. On the way here some awful station got onto our wavelength and tried to tune in. Its codesign was UQM and it went on saying 'Uncle Queen Mike', accentuating each word in turn – *UNCLE* Queen Mike, Uncle *QUEEN* Mike, Uncle Queen *MIKE*, and so on. Everyone got so fed up with it that most tank commanders started copying it and bedlam soon ensued on the wireless for most of the remainder of the march.

On 21 November after waking up to find all the windows had been broken by a close shell, the advance began again, our objective being the village of Tongerlo just south of Maasbree. B Squadron were on the right making for Schoorveld which was entered unopposed, and C Squadron on the left. I was on the left again with my Troop. We advanced without opposition through the wooded country and then remained in positions on the outskirts of the wood looking across the fields towards Tongerlo. C Squadron struck a lot of mines beside where we were and when the REs arrived I saw one get his foot blown off by a Schu anti-personnel mine. The night before we began this advance Colonel Tim had a message saying that Mary, his wife, was very ill having her baby so he flew home for a few days and left Frank to command. Brigadier Mike was speaking on the rear link wireless one day and asked to speak to 'Sunray' so Frank grabbed the microphone and politely answered, 'How Item, Sunray speaking, Sir, over.' Shortly afterwards the Brigadier lost his excellent Dingo driver when they went over a mine and the driver had a leg blown off.

B Squadron passed through us late in the afternoon and John Gunn controlled his Squadron magnificently across a very boggy patch of ground and captured a group of farms. It was this advance across what was thought to be non-tank country, which caused the enemy to withdraw from villages in the south. The following day the 60th put in an attack on Tongerlo supported by A Squadron and some flails. As soon as the village fell B and C Squadrons were concentrated round RHQ, as 44 RTR had converged across our front. A Squadron came back the following day. That morning I did a recce out to 15th Scottish Division on the left and met a patrol from their Recce Regiment. You could see their column of vehicles stretching for miles and consisting of bridge-laying Churchills and other types of vehicles. Ian Readman was shot through the chest while B Squadron was pulling out and had to be evacuated.

We were four days in this area and again Ted and I had found ourselves a room in a cottage which we shared with an old man of ninety, who luckily went off to his box bed early, pulled the curtains and left Ted and me in peace to play piquette in the room which was unbearably hot for there had been a roaring fire all day and only one tiny window that didn't open. It rained most of the time here and I found the best way of drying my shoes was to put them in the oven.

We left here on the 25th. It was just as well that we left for the old man was taken ill that morning – we thought probably from not being able to sleep the night before owing to the noise that Ted and I made playing 'racing demon'! Our route was via Beringen, past the 'Baker Sixteen' place (see beginning of this chapter), Nederweert, Zomeren to a small collection of houses about two miles to the south. I had led the Regiment as far as Nederweert and then was able to go ahead so as to get things prepared for the Troop when they arrived.

CHAPTER XXVII

Winter Quarters

On arrival at Zomeren on 25 November we were told that we would be there for a few days rest and to do some maintenance, so we got temporarily billeted in barns; but we might have known that it probably meant we would be there several months – in actual fact we remained in the same place for two and a half months.

During our stay there, many things happened and were done. The Python scheme came to a head and after several visits to Army HQ the Colonel eventually got a firm ruling that those who wished could take leave in lieu of Python – this was the first instance of LILOP which became so popular after the War – which meant they would get a month's leave and return to the Regiment while the others who took full Python got a month's leave and remained at home for a further two months, losing any acting or temporary rank. Sixty-four ORs – half those eligible – elected to take LILOP and returned a month later. Several of the Python men also returned after the War. Colonel Tim who was eligible for Python was not able to take it as Monty appointed him his GI RAC at Army Group, and it was a sad day when he left. Frank took over command and Hugh second-in-command; Ted Robinson went to B Squadron as second-in-command to John Gunn who became Squadron Leader and Tony Larcom[1] was posted to us as Technical Adjutant. He turned out to have been my Sergeant Instructor at Bovington when I was a cadet in 1940.

One of the first things Frank did on taking over command was to get rid of Johnnie Johnston, our doctor, who was amongst those who had just received a Military Cross. We were all very sorry at his departure for he was tremendously popular with both officers and other ranks and we thought he had done his job as RMO admirably during the two and a quarter years he had been with us. He went to 14 Light Field Ambulance where he became Brigadier Mike's right-hand man

---

1   Captain A. Larcom, Technical Adjutant.

and being still in the Brigade, he always remained a staunch friend of the Regiment.

Two days after arriving at Zomeren I heard that I, amongst others, had got the MC for the action we had on the Somme at Long. On 29 November we all went to a hall in Weert where Monty held an investiture and gave us our ribbons.

After a week or two when we realized we would be in the same place for some time, we got more settled in and comfortable. The RHQ Officers' Mess was in a school which was always freezing for the stove never worked except as a smoke screen. We had several dinners there including one or two Regimental ones which all officers

General Montgomery pinning on the ribbon referred to in the text

from Squadrons attended. Sgt Heron and his dance band played and he acted well when Colonel Frank called him over after 'The King' to have a drink. Cpl Benton, Mess Corporal, also gave us a lot of amusement. When he opened a bottle of champagne, he would gradually work the cork out by pushing it with his thumbs at the same time glancing at the spot on the ceiling where he reckoned it would hit. There would then be a loud explosion and the cork would go ricochetting round the room and usually land on the guest's head. One morning he came in and asked Richard for some brandy which he wanted for a pudding. Richard thought he would pull his leg, filled a glass and said, 'Yes of course, Cpl Benton, here you are, your good health.' Without a moment's hesitation, he quoffed it down much to Richard's surprise!

To keep our fire going at all, we used to go out to the woods with an axe and saw to get logs which were usually too green to burn. When I was out one day, I found a lot of beehives and a couple of boys who offered me some honey. I bought a lot and when I saw the boys run away with the money laughing, I realized that probably they had nothing to do with the hives at all. However I got the honey which was delicious, dark, rich, heather honey.

The winter was very hard on the whole and in January we had quite a bit of snow and hard frost. The tanks were unable to go along the roads as they merely slid off into the deep ditches each side. The day after a heavy blizzard my troop woke up in their barn to find a drift on top of them so we had to make an inner wall and roof of straw and tarpaulins. When the thaw came no vehicle was allowed on the roads for two or three days as the surfaces all started to sink in the wet and when a vehicle did go along, they moved up and down in waves, a most extraordinary sight. Because of the snow and frost, not much football could be played. Those fond of shooting had quite good sport after duck, partridge, blackgame etc., although we had no large bags. There were many geese about but usually on the move and we never had a shot at one. An officer's Eton Wall Game was played against 4th Armoured Brigade HQ at Leende which we lost 7-0.

It was just before Christmas that my brother-in-law, Willie Whitelaw, invited me to dine with the 3rd Battalion Scots Guards, of which he was 2i/c, in their commandeered 'club' in Eindhoven. Richard Shelley was also invited and luckily we borrowed the A Squadron staff car driven by Tpr Berry, for we had a tremendous evening dancing reels till 4 a.m. Berry assured us next day that he managed to get us to bed – he may be right for I certainly don't remember! I was in a bad way the next day when Sgt Donnan woke me up at some unearthly hour to say goodbye before setting off for UK on Python. Sgt O'Rourke arrived to take over as Troop Sergeant and I could not have been happier than to renew our close relationship, formed when he drove the Colonel's Dingo and me in Italy.

Christmas Day was celebrated in the traditional style. A church service, which was very well attended, was held in the large B Squadron barn, followed by men's dinners which were very good indeed. We had been lucky over every Christmas during the War for we were always out of the line and able to enjoy it. Hogmanay was also celebrated by the traditional Sergeants' Mess Smoker at which everyone was in good spirits. It was a small affair for many Sergeants had gone home on either LILOP or Python but even so, it was as good as any other. New

Year's Day, on the other hand, was not celebrated in the usual style for General Baker, GOC VIII Corps, decided to inspect us, a Scottish Regiment, on the one day in the year which a Scotsman calls his own. Everyone had to be up early cleaning, polishing and preparing. He must have thought us an ill lot of men for the majority had hangovers. Just before he arrived a special main guard was mounted under Sgt Chalmers and dismissed as soon as he left. They were very smart indeed, all white blanco and polished. He was very impressed with it and asked Sgt Chalmers if this was the normal guard. Keeping a straight face he told him we always had a 24-hour main guard mounted at RHQ.

We had several other inspections and visits, notably those by General Ritchie, GOC XII Corps on 7 December, General 'Pip' Roberts, GOC 11th Armoured Division on 27 December and by Mike Carver, our Brigadier, on 12 December. For the latter inspection, we were all beezed up in our best boots, anklets, battle dress etc., and were rather taken back when he arrived in gumboots, polo-neck sweater and old greatcoat for he had come essentially to inspect the tanks. He plunged through the deep mud followed closely by Colonel Frank who tried to step in his footprints before the mud flowed back in!

A training area was found only two miles away and I spent many days in this area of wood and heather doing schemes with the Recce Troop. We always took our food out and brewed up at one of the farms. One of these, called Grashut, was our favourite and great was our concern when, one day, we arrived to find half of it had been demolished by a bomb dropped the night before. I do not think there were any casualties which was fortunate for they were nice people. Everyone enjoyed going out and learnt a lot from it. One day we were having a peaceful brew outside a pub when my wireless picked up a faint message from RHQ, the only words of which I could make out were: 'You are to return at once.' This was shortly after the Ardennes flap when parachutists had been dropped at Army HQ not so very far away and I thought that, of course, there was a flap on and we were to move; so we all mounted and came back at a great rate of knots only to find that two of my tanks were to be handed into FDS in exchange for two new ones. We did not only use the training area for tank schemes for we also did dismounted schemes, mapped pieces of country and other useful exercises.

At the time of the Ardennes offensive the enemy carried out a large-scale air attack on airfields in Holland and Belgium and we saw a great number of enemy jet planes which flew very low, hedge-hopping in order not to be seen or fired at by our AA guns. During this time some B Squadron fitters, who were changing tracks on the road, were attacked by a burst of cannon shells fired by what was thought to have been one of our own Typhoons; three of them were wounded. A new invention reached us which was an extended end-connector on the tracks which made them about three inches wider. We put on two demonstrations of these for various local commanders to see. They were proved to be satisfactory and all our tanks were eventually fitted with them.

At the beginning of December we were told to prepare to take over a sector of the Maas front, so several of us went down there to recce it, the area being centred on the village of Thorn which was forward of Kinroy and known to us from previous days. Everything having been settled and the Regiment ready to move, it was cancelled.

During our time at Zomeren we all went on the ranges several times. During December we went to a large range at Lommel, which was some distance to the west of Weert. We spent a night on the way in some excellent billets in Loozen. Returning the next day meant a long detour via Walkenswaard for these roads were all one-way. Later Ken Baker[1] and I went off to see the CLY about a local range. I was driving the staff car which got stuck, so we shouted at some locals to give us a push and off we set again. When we got to our destination, we looked round and discovered that Cargill, the driver, was missing. Unknown to us, he had got out to push when we got stuck and we had left him behind. We went back for him but he had hitch-hiked home. This range was used a lot by all Squadrons and was very handy being only about three or four miles away.

Several schemes were carried out with 4 KSLI the far side of Nederweert. They took place in the ruined village of Huiyen and a Squadron did one day with a different company of infantry. I went down with Colonel Frank as a sort of umpire for only two sections of Recce Troop

---

1 Lieutenant K.T.W. Baker, Troop Leader.

were taking part and they came under direct command of the Squadron Leader.

At the beginning of February there were many rumours of us moving and taking part in the 'Battle of the Rhineland', which was to clear the country between the Maas and the Rhine. At the same time I heard that I was to go on one week's UK leave and I was not sure whether I would get away before we moved. However our impending move was postponed every day and I got off on leave on 14 February – four days before the Regiment moved.

I handed Recce Troop over to John Dawes, expecting to be back there in a week or two, but alas, that was not to be. I spent the first night with Tony Bonham at B Echelon where we wined and dined well. The next day I set off early to the Report Centre at Vaulville about ten miles from Weert. From here we were sent on to the Transit Camp at Bourg Leopold where we remained for the afternoon. I travelled back with Tpr Smith 25 who had been my tank driver almost continuously since December 1942 and was to become my jeep driver for another six months on his return to the Regiment; he was going on Python. From Bourg Leopold we went on an awful night journey by train to Calais where we found we had to remain for forty-eight hours as there had been two days' cancellation of sailing. When we left, we had a long walk to the docks and no porters, and my arms all but came out of their sockets carrying my very heavy case filled with champagne. I eventually got to Harwich and from there home by special train.

I only had a week's leave but, on my last day, my father had one of his bad goes and the Doctor advised me to stay, so I got a week's extension by which time he had improved, and back I set to the Regiment via Dover, Calais and Bourg Leopold where I found Mo Williams who was on his way to the Regiment, having been recalled from leave after only two days. There had been a few officer casualties and he had to return to take over his Squadron again. Luckily he had a jeep to collect him and knew where to go for, while I had been away, the Regiment had moved up to Nijmegen via Tilburg, taken part in the Battle of the Rhineland and was returning to Sonnis eight miles SW of Bree, the following day. This place was only a few miles away so we went there and found Hugh with the advance party. The following day, 9 March, the Regiment arrived. As I was walking across to the Recce

Troop to take it over again I was hailed by Colonel Frank who told me that I was to take over as Adjutant from John Warrender who had been hit over the head by a branch while sitting on top of his tank on a transporter. I was not at all pleased at the prospects as I had seen how hard an Adjutant had to work in battle and also how tied down he was, which did not at all suit me who had been used to swanning about all over the country in my previous jobs. However, I was told I had to and realized that it was certainly an honour to have been appointed. James Hanbury[1] took over Recce Troop.

We remained at Sonnis in some old barracks for a week and I gradually got into the ways of my new job. I had no takeover for John had gone to hospital for a day or two, but Orderly Room Sergeant Sullivan and his staff were very good and helpful. I was particularly struck by the willingness of my Orderly Room truck driver, Tpr Williams, who acted as general orderly. After the War I immediately got him as my jeep driver and later as servant. I could not have chosen a better man, always cheerful and willing and a very good cleaner of kit.

While I had been away the Regiment had been in one of its toughest battles and I must consider myself lucky that I missed it. On the way there they had several casualties in Tilburg when B Echelon was bombed. The fighting they took part in was just south of the Reichswald Forest immediately after it had been captured and their objective together with 4 KSLI was the village of Udem. For this operation, 4th Armoured Brigade had taken the place, in 11th Armoured Division, of 29th Armoured Brigade who had gone back to Belgium to get new tanks. As I was not in this battle I shall not attempt to describe it. There were three things about it that were on everyone's lips on returning: firstly, how marvellously Tom Mahoney had done when he suddenly had to take over A Squadron and how he had recced, under fire, an anti-tank ditch on foot looking for a crossing place – his tank was eventually brewed up and he was very severely burnt and wounded – I am glad to say he got a bar to his MC for this; secondly, what a very fierce battle it was; and thirdly how very well the KSLI had fought and how successfully they had co-operated with the Regiment, their Colonel being a cousin of Ted Robinson.

---

1 Captain J.R. Hanbury, Troop Leader.

A 'Brew-Up' before the Battle, 27 February 1945

After tea on 15 March I received a message that we were to move early next morning back to a concentration area at Udem prior to the Rhine crossing. I got into a bit of a flap as everyone had unpacked all their kit and it seemed that it would take us days to pack up again. However, everything always turns out alright in the end and we were ready to move at half-past ten except for Tpr Berry and my jeep which caught up later. I was quite excited for I should cross into Germany that night for the first time although the Regiment had crossed the frontier on 24 February. We went by transporter to Maasbree where we remained till midnight, then moved on our tracks via Venlo, Straelen, Geldern, Kevelar, Winnekendonk and Udem where we arrived at six-thirty in the morning feeling very hungry and sleepy.

CHAPTER XXVIII

Into Germany

We remained at Udem for a week and RHQ was billeted in some dirty little houses about half a mile outside the village while the Squadrons were on the edge of the village – A Squadron being in a shoe factory. The time here was spent in preparing for the next operation – the assault-crossing of the Rhine. On 22 March Brigadier Mike spoke to the Regiment and told us that our job was to cross, once the bridgehead had been formed, and then keep up the momentum of the attack; 44 RTR were crossing in DD tanks[1] in close support of 53rd (Welsh) Division, and the 6th Airborne Division were dropping the other side just after the initial assault which was to begin at 2200hrs on 23 March.

On the morning of the 24th the Colonel assembled all officers and explained in detail what our role would be. While this was going on the Airborne Division passed over us; it was an incredible sight, literally hundreds of planes and gliders going methodically across the Rhine, regardless of AA fire, dropping their load, turning round and returning over us. One glider was hit, disintegrated in mid-air and out fell a small Tetrarch tank – a terrible thing for the crew who, it was understood, were inside it. That evening we were all ready to move down to the river as we were supposed to cross at 2000hrs but it was postponed and we did not move till 0100hrs, when we proceeded very slowly via Labbeck to the Armoured Assembly Area situated in some lovely green fields behind the 'bund'. There we waited all day for there was much delay at the ferry until we received orders to cross the Class 40 pontoon bridge just north of Xanten at Bislich. We leaguered beside 2 KRRC on the other side of the river, the last Squadron not arriving till early in the morning.

The next three or four days were very sticky for the country was flat and heavily wooded and groups of enemy infantry, SPs and 20mm guns

---

1 Fitted with high canvas sides and propellers so they could float across rivers.

were continually being met. However, progress was made each day, and we passed through Haminkeln, Ringenburg and Dingden where we had to leave the roads and make our way by tracks across country. There were several minor engagements but no battle ever developed. We arrived at a place very late one night during which C Squadron was supporting an attack by 2 Monmouthshires and 4 RWF. There was a lot of spasmodic firing from the woods surrounding us so we all clustered round a small farm and leaguered for the night – or for the two hours that was left of it. In a room of the house we found a large pile of eiderdowns so Colonel Frank, Colonel Chris Consett, Hugh and myself threw ourselves down on it anyhow and slept like logs inspite of our feet sticking in each other's faces. We had nearly emerged out of the woods onto the main road running east from Bocholt and there was only one area still holding out which the infantry were unable to clear, so Sgt Donnan in his Stuart tank quite calmly drove into this piece of wood, drove round the enemy positions and out again, quite unmoved. This little trip of his soon made the enemy withdraw and he got a well-earned MM for it.

On 29 March Mirleees Chassels left the Regiment and David took over A Squadron. During the afternoon there were a lot of discussions between Colonel Frank and Hugh after the former had returned from seeing Brigadier Mike. I was told to gather Squadron Leaders and when they arrived the Colonel announced to us all in a stentorian voice: 'I've got the bowler hat.' We knew it wasn't a proper 'bowler hat' he had got but he was going because he was a very tired man and it was considered that the next pursuit across Germany would be too much for him. He was very moved and exceedingly sorry to go. While all this was going on, a message came to say there was an enemy SP about 500 yards away. This was confirmed from several sources, so Frank, typical of his fearlessness, announced to us that, as his last act before leaving, he was going to look for this thing to see if it was really there, so off he set in his burberry and glasses over his shoulder, armed with a pistol, to seek out the enemy SP. He would not let any of us go with him and we were indeed glad when he returned sometime after and reported nothing there. He then got into the staff car and after a tender farewell to us all he drove off. Hugh took over command only temporarily for he had applied for Duggie to come back from the Staff College to take over. Mo Williams came to RHQ as Second-in-Command and Ted took over C Squadron.

On 30 March our orders were to pass through Bocholt which had just fallen and pursue the enemy north-eastwards. On entering Bocholt many mines were encountered and Colonel Chris Consett's scout car was blown up; he was injured and had to be evacuated. The advance proceeded without opposition through Rhede. Just north of this place we were held up by a blown bridge which was too wide for the Scissors bridge so Recce Troop found a way round and David's Squadron was passed through again. When David got back on to the centre line, he lost his bearings and turned the wrong way, soon coming face to face with the blown bridge on the other side! We were supposed to go on to Oding but it was learnt that the 8th Hussars were attacking this place so we were stopped near Borkenwirthe to let them carry out their operation. During the night a message came via Brigade HQ from HQ 7th Armoured Division to say that the 8th were nowhere near us. We protested and told them we had an LO with them who confirmed they were where we thought they were, but they still would not believe us so Ken Baker was sent off and he found them exactly where we said. When they had cleared this area we went on to Oding but there was such a muddle of vehicles from us and from 7th Armoured Division that the Brigadier told us and the 60th to find somewhere to stop and carry out maintenance, so we dispersed in some very nice farms where we replenished our ration boxes with hams, eggs, and anything else we found. The inhabitants in the RHQ farm were exceedingly 'bolshy' and we had to turn them all out into a cottage as the army policy was that we were not to share houses with them.

After stopping here for one night we received our orders for the next advance which was to be in a north-easterly direction through Vreden and Ahaus. We crossed back into Holland for the night near Winterswijk. It was extraordinary the respect the troops showed for the Dutch, for, during the few previous nights, they had been in Germany and had done a lot of looting and now they had only gone about a mile into Holland and never touched a thing. On the way there RHQ crossed a very flimsy, wooden and steel-girder bridge. The first two tanks got over alright; the bridge sank about two feet in the middle as Robin Dunn's tank (C Battery Commander, 4 RHA) crossed and then collapsed all together as Sgt O'Connel's tank crossed. He managed to get out with a tow and the remaining vehicles had to find another way round.

The advance on 2 April went very quickly through Stadtlohn, Vreden, Ottenstein, Epe and Ochtrup where considerable opposition, chiefly small arms, was encountered on the line of the railway and in a large factory. The Recce Troop had led all the way and at Epe, James, who was in the leading tank troop of the Brigade, so he thought, was rather puzzled when he found his route marked with the Brigade centre-line signs; but he eventually caught up a military police jeep which had been miles ahead of everyone quite calmly signing the route. The occupants got a bit of a shock when James said, 'My dear old thing, do you realize I'm the leading tank of the Brigade?' It soon got dark when we arrived at Ochtrup and things came to a standstill and got rather unpleasant, no one knowing whether to expect the enemy to withdraw or to attack them. Supported by B Squadron, the 60th put in an attack on the factory and appeared to clear it. One of the B Squadron tanks fell through the road surface into a stinking sewer, much to the crew's concern. RHQ and Battalion HQ of the 60th made a small pub their headquarters and there was great excitement when one of the guard fired a magazine from his Sten at a movement in the wood which turned out to be cow which he missed!

The next morning everything was quiet again and we had orders to come under command 52nd (Lowland) Division who were in Neuen-kirchen, whence we proceeded via Metelen and Wettringen. Duggie arrived back in the Regiment that day and took over command. He had only had a day or two's notice to pack up in the middle of his Staff College course to come out and take over.

We spent two nights in very comfortable houses in Neuenkirchen waiting for the crossing of the Dortmund-Ems Canal. While here C Squadron did a small operation helping to clear the airfield and some woods to the north of Rheine which they did successfully. One tank was knocked out and one of the crew was killed but opposition on the whole was light and Mo took two of the objectives himself in his Dingo. A Squadron moved down to the canal on the 5 April and assisted the Glasgow Highlanders to cross and later that day, after the usual orders, counter-orders, postponements and delays, the remainder of the

Regiment concentrated on the eastern outskirts of Rheine preparatory to crossing the canal the following day and continuing the advance. RHQ and Recce got a block of flats as billets and as usual made the occupants double up in one of them, leaving the remainder free. We could not make up our minds which flat to put the Germans into. There was a choice of two: one with a bed-ridden old lady and a mass of dirty grandchildren, or one which had a crippled lunatic youth. We decided to put the Germans with the old lady and keep the lunatic in a room by himself. We thought afterwards that he may have been no lunatic at all but merely a fifth columnist shamming!

On 6 April we crossed the canal and our objective with 156 Brigade was Hopsten village. The village of Dreierwalde was captured first after slight resistance and a delay was caused by a blown bridge which had to be spanned by a Bailey. B Squadron had attacked up the main road and on a parallel track to the left while the remainder of the Regiment went up the track to the right and remained there while the bridge was put up, managing a quick breakfast and shave. As soon as we crossed over, the advance went quickly till the approaches to Hopsten which appeared to be quite strongly defended by SP and A/Tk guns. B Squadron lost one tank which was immobilized on a mine and then shot twice by an A/Tk gun through the engine, setting it on fire. We made RHQ in a farm on the edge of the airfield; this was not very comfortable as there was not a pane of glass in the house and to make matters worse, my tummy kept me on the run, having to visit the garden in the rain every quarter of an hour with my shovel! The following evening A Squadron moved over to prepare for an attack that night on Recke with a company of 6th Cameronians. The attack started soon after midnight but there was no opposition and by dawn they had occupied the village.

On the 8th we moved up through Hopsten and Halverde to a concentration area whence C Squadron could advance to capture their objective which was two bridges just north of Voltlage. That evening Duggie and I went forward in the jeep to visit B Squadron and watched an attack by rocket-firing Typhoons on an enemy-held wood. It was a most exciting and impressive sight. The following day C Squadron gained their objectives without opposition and we leaguered in Voltlage in a very attractive old half-timbered farmhouse, which, I am afraid to say, lost some of its beauty after the Churchill bridgelayer had gone into the garden! We supplemented our rations here with a very fat young pig. From here we moved on via Merzen to Uffeln where we found a colony of farms in a wood where the Regiment concentrated, except for A Squadron who were still advancing to the east of us and took Alfhausen and Bersenbruck on the following day. Here David made his HQ in a very nice hotel and got some excellent wine from the cellars. On the way to Uffeln we passed two holes in the road in which were placed large aerial bombs set so as to go off like mines. Luckily these were discovered before they blew anything up and we were able to by-pass them. C Squadron in the meantime had been told to proceed in the middle of the night by a roundabout route along tracks to occupy Holdorf with a company of infantry and to contact 53 Recce Regiment.

RHQ moved on to a farm just north of Alfhausen where the Squadrons congregated later. The farmer and his family locked themselves up in the attic and we had great difficulty in getting him down to help one of his cows which was having difficulties calving and had woken us all up. Hugh had been at Holdorf with C Squadron and returned to RHQ with a local pattern fire engine full of every sort of firearm which he had captured or looted. Tpr Stringer was given the fire engine to make into a staff car for Hugh, and Ken Baker, the RIO, had the pleasure of destroying all the guns. Just before midnight on the 12th we moved with 52nd Division on a seventy-mile march to an area south of Bremen. During this march we were diverted off to rejoin 4th Armoured Brigade which we reached via Diepholz and Sulingen at 8 a.m. near Asendorf, after a very tiring and long night march. We expected to be here forty-eight hours but were rather annoyed when we heard we should be moving at 6 a.m. the following morning, so we got in as much maintenance and sleep as we could.

Meanwhile 44 RTR had crossed the River Aller at Rethem early that day and we had to follow them so as to pass through in the evening. Our route crossed the Weser at Hoya and then by tracks through the wood to the south-east till we were halted together with 6 RWF (Royal Welch Fusiliers) at the village of Stocken where we remained for several hours till the situation on the east of the Aller cleared up. Everyone was very exhausted and the fields were littered with sleeping bodies.

We eventually got the word to cross at Rethem, so we all moved slowly forward. At first only Tac RHQ and C Squadron crossed because, 44 RTR having been held up by various demolitions, there was not room for more till things had started to move. A and B Squadrons then crossed and Main RHQ stayed in Rethem with Recce Troop. RHQ was in a dentist's house alongside the railway siding in which was an abandoned train fitted with heavy AA guns. Our 'Ops Room' was in the consulting room and when the officer and operator on duty were bored with looking at all the false teeth, they could rest comfortably on the dentist's chair, tipped to the required angle!

In order to advance to Kirchboitzen, which was our next objective, it was necessary to go through a thick wood at night which was held by a German Marine Regiment with Panzerfausts and Spandaus. Duggie split up the Regiment and the infantry Battalion into Coy/Sqn groups and gave orders that groups were to leapfrog each other from track to track, the tanks proceeding in line ahead up the centre-line track followed by the infantry in Kangaroos, and both tanks and Kangaroos firing their machine-guns into the wood directly past the side of the vehicles in front, setting fire to the undergrowth. In this novel way all opposition melted and the far side of the wood was reached with no casualties. First light found the Sqn/Coy groups in a depression on the high ground near Klein Eilstorf and A Squadron, with two companies, immediately put in an attack on Kirchboitzen. There was some slight disorganization with the infantry and Alec Lewis, who had two troops under him, found himself on the outskirts of the village without them, so he decided to go on and reached the centre much to the concern of the defenders who, in their alarm, fired a salvo of six Panzerfausts at Dennis Andrews and missed! RHQ in the meantime had crossed the Aller and after a halt at Altenwahlingen had joined Tac RHQ and the Squadrons, who were replenishing just west of Kirchboitzen after having been relieved by 3 RTR. Duggie put Tac RHQ in a small orchard where he proudly displayed an anti-tank gun and two prisoners captured by himself!

Our next orders were to strike due north and cut the main road running east from Verden which we were trying to outflank. The first village on the route, Vethem, was strongly held by infantry with Panzerfausts. Recce Troop found a way over the stream to the east of the village and spotted four 105mm guns which were engaged and destroyed by B Squadron who had followed the Stuarts round. It was then decided that the village would be simultaneously attacked from the south by A Squadron and from the east by B and C Squadrons. However, owing to bad going this attack was not successful so, to save time, C Squadron with two companies of infantry in Kangaroos, the whole commanded by Tac RHQ, advanced north again and captured Idsingen without opposition. In the meantime A Squadron had pulled back from Vethem and shelled the place in order to drive out the infantry who were well concealed in the buildings. This was partially successful and B Squadron was able to enter and clear it up. During this latter part poor Johnnie Briggs[1] was killed in his tank by a sniper. One of our best junior officers, his loss was a great blow to the Regiment and was felt by everyone, especially myself, for I had got to know him well while he was in RHQ and when, at Zomeren, we had gone shooting and for walks together for no one was more fond of the country than he. He was buried that night by A1 Echelon in Kirchboitzen and after the War his grave was removed to the large military cemetery on the Celle–Soltau road.

B Squadron and the remainder of the infantry spent the night in Vethem and RHQ and A Squadron stayed outside. Early the next morning we heard over the air that an enemy horsed transport column had tried to enter Idsingen, supposed by them to be still held by Germans, but had been shot up by Sgt Wentzell's troop and had lost twenty men, several horses and three 105mm guns. While C Squadron continued the advance towards Bendingbostel (known by us as 'Brenda's Brothel') RHQ and the remainder of the Regiment and the infantry followed on to Idsingen. Just north of this place the Recce Troop came across a blown bridge and a lot of sniping. One of the tank turrets got stuck, so Tpr Liddell, the operator, got out to clear it. He was sniped and then Sgt Donnan and LCpl Taylor both got sniped while assisting Liddell. They were all shot in the legs and evacuated. After laying a Churchill bridge and making a log road across the boggy ground the advance was continued without opposition through Gr. and Kl. Heins to the main road. While the whole column was waiting to move on the odd enemy infantryman would appear and give himself

---

1 Lieutenant J. Briggs, Troop Leader.

up or the more audacious ones would take pot-shots at vehicles – not very pleasant.

During the afternoon the final attack on Bendingbostel was put in. There were two small woods covering the entrance to the village and these were held by the enemy who had an 88mm gun, as reported by a Belgian POW. The infantry attacked these woods across the main road and were immediately fired on by the gun. C Squadron tanks engaged it and knocked it out, thus clearing the way to the village which was soon occupied. A Squadron passed through to Brunsbrock and patrolled north of the railway where a tank got stuck. The rest of the Regiment remained in Bendingbostel, C Squadron having to evacuate their billets in a hurry in the middle of the night as they suddenly burst into flames. The RHQ house was a store of clothing, eiderdowns etc., many of the latter still gracing the beds of some officers! During the night one shell landed on the HQ fitter's half-track and wounded Tpr Hedges who died soon afterwards.

The following day we started off at first light, picked up A Squadron at Brunsbrock and passed through 44 RTR who were at Kreepen. As we passed A Squadron, David was sitting on his tank glaring at some petrified German prisoners standing rigidly to attention below him. These prisoners had been sleeping in the attic of the house in which Dennis's[1] troop had spent the night. He never discovered them till the morning complete with arms and ammunition. Recce Troop then led us on through Deelsen to the high ground at Scharnhorst where we could see the top of the church spire at Verden. On the way here Dennis had a conversation on the telephone through an interpreter with the German Commander of the nearby village of Langwedel, and was arranging for his surrender when he was cut off. There was a long unexplained wait here and everyone took the opportunity for a brew and a walk with a shovel. While busy with the latter, Major Kinahan, commanding the Kangaroo[2] Squadron, was straddled by a Nebelwefer stonk; he soon came running back hitching his trousers up but none the worse! By midday C Squadron had moved on to cut the road running north from Verden and had met a lot of enemy in some woods

1 Lieutenant D.J. Andrews, Troop Leader.
2 A tracked Armoured Personnel Carrier.

on a piece of high ground near Neumuhlen. Duggie and I had followed them up in his Stuart and watched C Squadron having great fun by first of all stonking the wood, then driving along broadside about fifty yards from them shouting to them to surrender; when they did not, the whole Squadron fired a belt of Browning at them and had another go; eventually they gave themselves up except for one man who was seen lying in a trench feigning to be dead with his hand on his gun. Someone saw him move so when he would not surrender, he was finished off. During this little party, some infantry had tried to escape round the end of the wood and were shot at. One of them was wounded and lay in the field unable to move. We were going to collect him afterwards but I am ashamed to say we completely forgot. I hope the cottage nearby took him in. There were a lot of hares and a few roe running about amongst the tanks and when people were bored with shooting Germans they tried their skill at game with very little success. This was the first time I had managed to get away from RHQ for a 'swan' since becoming Adjutant, and I never enjoyed anything more. We returned that night to very comfortable billets in the Burgermeister's house at Deelsen.

The next day A Squadron continued the advance on Bremen and after some opposition they captured Langwedel. The concrete and rubble road blocks there had to be blown away by gunfire. The remainder of the Regiment moved to Neumuhlen preparatory to continuing the advance the next day. The road to Bremen was heavily defended, chiefly by 88mm Flak guns, originally used as part of the town's AA defence. C Squadron passed through A Squadron and captured Etelsen after a bit of opposition; Mo made the Schloss his headquarters, which must have been a large German HQ for the place was full of office equipment and stationery of which my Orderly Room made full use. RHQ moved up to Langwedel for the night and we had to mount a strong guard over a house where many crates of red wine had been found. There was a certain amount of shelling coming from the woods to the north of the road so A Squadron was sent through them with the Glasgow Highlanders and approached Etelsen from the north, Dennis losing a tank on the way. The next objective was the village of Baden which C Squadron captured on 21 April after some opposition from an 88mm and snipers, the usual effective defence in these villages. During the following day the Regiment concentrated and carried out maintenance. We were all in a group of nice houses and everyone managed to get a good wash, the first for a few days. The following day, B Squadron took up the advance and after the usual opposition captured Achim. On the main road outside the village there were several large aerial bombs buried in the road and connected by a fuze to a dugout, where a German sat waiting for a tank or other vehicles to cross over it and then set it off. Two 'Crocodiles'[1] were blown up and, to show the force of the explosion, they were blown right over onto their turrets in the garden at the side of the road. RHQ moved up straight behind so as to be in Achim ready for the final advance to Bremen. There was rather a muddle on the way as we kept being told to stop, then go on, then turn round and, with RHQ, A1 Echelon and all the hangers on, there was quite a considerable party, but with the help of LCpl Farquhar, my DR, I got things more or less sorted out and eventually we got into some houses in Achim, where orders and counter-orders were received for the capture and entry of Bremen.

On 24 April, C Squadron advanced into Bremen against ever-fading resistance and had established themselves in the centre by midday. Two of John Althorp's tanks were knocked out and he had quite a tricky time getting back on foot with a lot of German soldiers running about the houses, shouting at him; Tpr Burns (later SSM) did very well as John's driver and managed to reverse the tank to the side of the road while it was burning so as not to block it. He got his MM there. Sgt Edgar and a troop of B Squadron were guarding a crossroads when a civilian crawled up unseen and, firing a Panzerfaust, knocked out his tank. 8th Armoured Brigade were still battling in the area of the large park on our right where the remaining defence of the town was centred round a General and the Bishop who had set up their Headquarters in a concrete air-raid shelter. 44 RTR passed through us to the dock area and we were told to concentrate and carry out maintenance, so we all got good billets in some large town houses each of which had a good and varied cellar. A German ambulance was seen driving along the street so it was halted, the back opened and it was found to be full of very good wine, being immediately 'requisitioned' by B Squadron. Duggie and I crawled through the smashed window of a looted chemist's

---

1 Flail mine-clearing tank.

shop and from the consulting room of the Doctor upstairs had a good view of the country to our right, but we could see nothing of the fighting which had been our object. We had expected to be in Bremen about a week and made ourselves comfortable; the Orderly Room had unpacked and set up shop in the house and the Mess was got going, but after two days we were on the move again to join the 60th at Bassen where our task was to be to push north to the Cuxhaven area. However, on arrival, this task was cancelled and the next day we were told to join 6th Airborne Division in the Lüneburg area. The first day we got to Eversen midway between Verden and Rotenburg and all the fields at dusk were full of roe-deer – I've never seen so many together. We spent that night in a tiny cottage and moved the next morning seventy miles via Rotenburg, Scheessel, Fintel, Insel, Einem, Wilsede, Dohle and Raven to Eyendorf, where A Squadron stopped, and on to Putensen where the remainder of the Regiment halted. The journey was chiefly by track across the large 'heides' or flat moors. Near Fintel we got into some trouble at a small bridge which gave way after several tanks had crossed, but another way was soon found. We arrived about 5 p.m. and great excitement was caused at RHQ by someone finding a case containing an SS Captain's uniform, buried in the garden. Evidently the son of the house had been in the SS and the family were terrified that they would all be shot. We then set to work looking for anything which might be buried and eventually unearthed several large jars of pickled eggs, sugar and lard which were very welcome. As soon as a line was laid to Brigade HQ, Brigadier Mike rang up and I was the unfortunate one who answered. He was furious that our tanks had made such a mess of a corner near Eyendorf and told us to get it mended straight away. The CLYs had gone that way as well so I got onto their Adjutant and together we sent a working party there who must have done the job well for the Brigadier was in good humour when we next saw him.

CHAPTER XXIX

Across the Elbe to the Baltic – and Peace!

There were many rumours as to what the next operation would be but it was generally known that we would be crossing the Elbe and making a dash somewhere. The next day C Squadron moved off to come under command of the Grenadier Armoured Battalion and got over the Elbe by a pontoon bridge at Lauenburg, having been straddled on the way. The rest of the Regiment remained another day till 1 May when Colonel Duggie, in the RIO's Stuart tank, and Recce Troop, moved on ahead in order to cross the bridge that day. After passing through Lüneburg they pulled off the road onto the racecourse and the whole of 11th Armoured Divisional column which was following did likewise. However, when this other column discovered that Recce Troop were only having breakfast, they realized their mistake and moved on. The traffic control at the bridge was very strict and would only allow those vehicles to cross which belonged to 11th Armoured Division so the Colonel told the Recce Troop to split into pairs and mix themselves up with the other tanks. This they did and managed to cross and get to Boizenburg with no questions being asked.

In the meantime I had taken RHQ, A and B Squadrons to a concentration area at Adendorf just beyond Lüneburg. At a crossroads in the latter place where I should have turned left, I was not allowed to as it was 'one-way' so I had to go straight on past the airfield which, with all its new concrete roads, was not marked on my map. I began to get lost and was not sure how near we were to the front so I kept going left to where we should be and eventually found myself in Nutzfelde which I found on my map. It was then only a short distance through Scharnebeck and Erbstorf. Hugh had gone ahead, and, as usual, had found us excellent billets. While we were all parked on the road waiting to pull in the Brigadier passed and, as usual, I was the wretched person at whom he let fly about all our 'captured' civilian cars, including Hugh's fire engine, which he said were blocking all the roads. I promised I would get rid of them straight away – I think we had them for another month!

None of us really knew what was happening as we had had no word from Duggie who was miles away, so we all went to bed expecting a message to arrive. At three in the morning, I was woken up by 'Dear old thing, are you awake?' This was James having come the whole way back in his 'Weasel' from Duggie with our orders. He was unable to cross the bridge over the Elbe against the traffic so had swum it in his 'Weasel'. The orders he brought were for us to leave at first light for the American bridge at Bleckede where we had priority. Dennis had already received this message in morse but Duggie had been unable to hear the acknowledgement owing to the bad wireless, so had sent James.

So on 2 May 1945 we commenced our last march of the War. Our route was via Neetze, over the bridge at Bleckede, to just short of Boizenburg then to Bengerstorf where we all halted for breakfast and for further orders. As we set off that morning we passed Tony Bonham outside B Echelon looking very tired, having never gone to bed that night as they had arrived very late, and Ted Acres who had a very bad attack of poisoning, was more or less unconscious and could not do anything. Nevertheless Tony gave us a cheery wave. At breakfast a lot of released prisoners came up to us overjoyed at being free and seeing the British Army. Even the Germans appeared pleased to see us for they were glad it was us and not the Russians, whom they dreaded. Meanwhile the 1st Canadian Parachute Regiment were mounted on the back of C Squadron tanks, and they had commenced the advance to Wismar on the Baltic at first light. The telephone between the War Office and 21 Army Group hummed all morning about the necessity to reach the Baltic, thereby preventing the Russians from getting to Denmark. 11th Armoured Division were therefore directed on Lübeck and 6th Airborne Division with ourselves on Wismar. I hoped that we might reach Wittenburg that day but it was entered unopposed at half-past ten in the morning and Gadebusch one and a half hours later. The remainder of the Regiment was about four hours behind C Squadron and were going flat out, trying to catch up. The sight on the road was amazing for there was no resistance, the enemy's only thought being to escape from the Russians; consequently we first met all their base workshops and Corps HQs coming streaming down the road in good order, the infantry marching in three's and the vehicles in convoy. Generals were sitting upright in their cars being driven by their ADCs. Gradually one got nearer the fighting troops who were acting as rearguard to this endless column retreating from our 'Allies'. Most of the German soldiers brought their wives or mistresses for whom there were special 'Families' Buses'. The order of march of our column was Recce Troop, the Colonel in his Dingo, 3 Para Brigade Commander on a DR's pillion, then C Squadron, and when Sgt Randall arrived at the level crossing at Bobitz he found a trainload of SP across it. He was told not to knock out the engine as that would block the road. The train soon moved on and when Duggie saw another approaching he stuck his Dingo across the line and stopped it. The Recce Troop rushed on to Wismar where all the barriers across the roads were down. This did not delay them as the civilians soon pushed them away allowing them to drive in, and in so doing we reached the Baltic. Duggie noticed a lot of low-flying planes so set out with two sections of Recce Troop to find the aerodrome which they soon came across outside the town. Here there was great excitement, some Germans rushing up to surrender, as pleased as Punch, and others starting to fire at our tanks till they discovered they were British and came up to apologize, having mistaken them for Russians. Duggie caught a lorry-load of soldiers getting away so gave them a burst of fire from his Sten which soon made them change their minds. C Squadron and their infantry arrived and took up positions round the town, the latter all remarking: 'I never knew tanks could go as fast as that.' By this time the remainder of the Regiment had arrived and John Gunn and his Squadron had great fun collecting a lorry-load of pistols from a hospital train at Bobitz. At nine o'clock that night, two scout cars and two motorcycle combinations drove in from the east manned by Russian troops of both sexes armed with Tommy guns and demanding the way to Denmark. They were very disappointed that we had cut off their line of advance but soon drowned their sorrows in vodka!

And so, on 2 May 1945, we ended the War with a grand hunt of a sixty-mile point and at least eighty as the Hun ran, and with the honour of being the first British troops to meet the Russians.

✦ ✦ ✦

Our Regimental Thanksgiving Service at the farm near Wismar, 8 May 1945

How did we feel now that the War in Europe was so suddenly over after nearly six years? It was difficult to describe but I think it was with a sense of relief, and thankfulness that we were alive while many of our friends were not. Therefore immediately the Armistice was signed we held an informal thanksgiving service on 8 May in the garden at RHQ, taken by 'Wee Mac', the Padre, who had sustained us and shared our travails the whole way from Egypt. This was not a parade but entirely voluntary and very many came from the outlying Squadrons, all with that same sense of relief and thankfulness. Later, on 27 May, we held a formal Remembrance Service for all who lost their lives in the Regiment. This was in the little German church near RHQ who had moved to a bigger and more suitable farm.

Epilogue

From Wismar, which became part of the Russian Zone, we moved five times in thirteen months, all over the British Zone – to Rotenburg near Bremen, to Lintfort west of the Rhine, to Husum near the Danish border, to Münster and finally in July 1946 to Lüneburg, thirty miles south-east of Hamburg, where we remained for five and a half years. As Adjutant, I got quite adept at movement orders!

After the War, I decided to stay in the Army and was granted a regular commission in the Regiment. In September 1946, I gave up as Adjutant and did various jobs in HQ Squadron – one of the first was to go back to Edinburgh with a 10-ton lorry and three soldiers to collect the regimental property. I became Band President; they had reformed and joined the Regiment in 1947, the same year as we inherited the Pipes and Drums from 52 Recce Regiment (ex-KOSB) and I became Pipe President, taking both Bands on a tour of Holland in 1949. They had already given a broadcast concert in the Hamburg Opera House in 1947 with both Bands playing together, setting a fashion which culminated in their winning a 'Golden Disc' and topping the charts in 1972 with 'Amazing Grace'.

In 1950, I went to B Squadron as second-in-command to Alec Lewis and the following year I was given command of C Squadron, spending more than three happy and adventurous years with them.

In 1952, we moved to Barce (El Merj), sixty miles north of Benghazi in Libya – a wonderful situation in the foothills of the Jebel Akdar with a dry hot summer and rain in the winter when the countryside sprang into colourful life. From there I took C Squadron to Malta for two weeks of exercises with the Marine Commandos – the first heavy tanks to be seen on the Island – and then for two three-month stints on detachment in the Canal Zone, and another three-month stint at Ma'an in Jordan, one of my happiest periods.

In 1953 I was lucky enough to be chosen to go home with our small regimental detachment to march in the Queen's Coronation Procession.

Immediately after that we went to the Remount Depot at Melton Mowbray to draw our horses and train as a mounted detachment under Michael Borwick,[1] to take part in the Queen's Coronation Visit to Edinburgh.

In January 1955, the Regiment went home to Crookham in Hampshire and I went as Training Officer to our affiliated Yeomanry – The Ayrshire Yeomanry – where the permanent staff were all Greys and where I made a lot of friends – a most enjoyable eighteen months.

Then I returned to the Regiment which took over the role of RAC Training Regiment at Catterick, and I became second-in-command to Michael Borwick and then to Alec Lewis. Under the latter, we returned in 1958 once more to Germany and an operational role at Münster, in our old barracks of 1946. In July 1959, I had the privilege of being appointed to command the Regiment, the ambition of any regimental officer. In June 1960, I moved them to an excellent barracks in the charming Westphalian town of Detmold in the foothills of the Teutoberger Wald. My two and a half years in command, besides being such an honour, were the greatest fun and I trust I handed over the Regiment to Jock Balharrie in January 1962 in as good a shape as when I took over. Our handover certificate is shown as being signed at 'Hotel Caspar Badrutt, St Moritz' where we were both staying as part of the Regimental Ski Team!

I was sad leaving the regimental family after living, working and fighting with them for twenty-one years. Luckily my last days at Detmold were cheered up during a very cold spell when about twenty of all ranks, armed with hockey sticks and a wooden puck, found a frozen farm pond where we played 'fun' ice-hockey each afternoon. However, that fun did not prevent a very large lump in my throat developing while giving my farewell address to the Regiment – I hope they understood.

---

1   Major M.G. Borwick, 2i/c Regiment.

Postscript

My uncle, Duncan Hay, asked if I would, on retirement from the Army, go back and help him to run his estate at Haystoun, just outside Peebles, as he was kindly making me his heir. It was wonderful news to know that I had something to do when I left the Regiment. I also knew that I would have to work hard, not only on the one large hill farm that was in hand, but two more were likely to come back in hand within a few years. With that prospect, I reckoned I had better have a proper holiday, so in February 1962 I set off by car to drive round the Mediterranean, crossing from Syracuse to Tripoli, then via Egypt, Jordan, Lebanon, Syria, Turkey, Greece, Yugoslavia, Austria and home – 14,000 miles and three months. This was a great experience and I am glad I took the opportunity, because it was some years before I got more than a week away. As expected, by 1969, I was farming three farms, with two others being let. As I wanted to enter into the community life, I made myself 'twelfth man' in the farm team, always helping at stock-handling and with the hay and harvest. That gave me time to become County Director of the Red Cross, County Commissioner of the Scouts, a County Councillor, active member of the various local agricultural committees and other such activities. One therefore got a good knowledge of the County. This was most helpful when, to my great surprise and pleasure, I was appointed in 1980 Lord Lieutenant of the County (now reverted to its old name of Tweeddale). In spite of all these jobs keeping me fairly busy, I still kept up with the Regiment whose Home Headquarters are in Edinburgh Castle, and I was for five years Chairman of the Edinburgh Branch of the Old Comrades becoming Vice-President of the Association some years later. I was also able to keep in touch with the Army when, in 1963, I took on the job of starter at the Army ski races on Cairngorm, doing it for the next thirty-three years.

As Lord Lieutenant one is required to retire on one's 75th birthday. A month or two earlier the District Council of Tweeddale, much to my astonishment, wished to make me a Freeman of the County with the Freedom Ceremony on my birthday. It was a wonderful and humbling occasion in the big Burgh Hall in Peebles; this was quite an emotional event for me, but nothing compared to what met my eyes when I left the Hall. Completely unbeknown to me, the Regiment had done me the honour of sending up from Catterick both the Military Band and the Pipes and Drums, and there they were welcoming me with 'Happy Birthday to You'. As tears welled up in my eyes and finding it hard to speak, they changed into 'Highland Cathedral', and then marched me down the High Street with the County Convener and Colonel Simon Allen, the Commanding Officer, who so kindly and secretly laid all this on.

What a day! To be honoured by both one's local County and by the Regiment – the two communities one had tried to serve over the years – was a wonderful experience, the more so being completely unexpected.

Regimental Officers mentioned in the text (final ranks, etc. shown)

ACRES, Major (QM) E.J. (Ted), MBE. Joined 1919 as Band boy. Commissioned Lieutenant Quartermaster 1941. Retired 1952.

ALTHORP, Captain Viscount, John, later Earl Spencer. Troop Leader.

ANDREWS, Major Dennis J., MC, later Nevison-Andrews. Troop Leader.

ARTHUR, Lieutenant Colonel Hon. Matthew, OBE, later Lord Glenarthur. Aged 31 on commissioning in 1940 and after joining the Regiment in 1941, he excelled on higher formation staff for the rest of the War.

BAKER, Major K.T.W. (Ken). Troop Leader. Regimental Intelligence Officer (RIO).

BERGER, Colonel O.C. (Ollie). Troop Leader, then Staff.

BODLEY, Lieutenant Mark C. Troop Leader, RIO. Killed in action (KIA) 1942.

BONHAM, Major Sir Anthony L.T., Bart. Troop Leader. 'B' Echelon Second-in-Command (2I/C).

BORWICK, Lieutenant Colonel Michael G. Joined Commandos. POW 1941. CO 1954–57.

BORWICK, Major Peter M., MC. Squadron 2I/C. Squadron Leader.

BOWLBY, Lieutenant Colonel F.E.S. (Frank), MC. Adjutant. Squadron Leader. Commanding Officer (CO) 1944–45.

BRASSEY, Colonel Sir Hugh T., KCVO, OBE, MC. Squadron Leader. Honorary Colonel Royal Scots Dragoon Guards 1973–79.

BRIGGS, Lieutenant J.S. (Johnnie). Troop Leader. KIA 1945.

CALLANDER, Major J. David, MC. Troop Leader. Squadron Leader.

CAYZER, The Captain Hon. M. Anthony R. (Tony). Troop Leader. Contracted Polio 1943.

CHASSELS, Captain Mirrlees, MC, also known as 'Chas'. Troop Leader. Squadron 2I/C.

COMPTON, Captain Alwyne A., MC. Later Farquharson of Invercauld. Troop Leader. Squadron 2I/C. Wounded 1944.

DAWES, Captain John S., MC. Troop Leader. Squadron 2I/C.

DE SALES LA TERRIERE, Lieutenant F.J.R. (Rory). Troop Leader. Died of wounds 1944.

DOWNIE, Captain Peter, REME. Officer I/C Light Aid Detachment, attached to Regiment 1941–44.

DUDGEON, Captain Ian H., MC. Troop Leader. Wounded 1944.

DUDGEON, Lieutenant Colonel J.H. (Joe). Pre-War Squadron Leader. 2I/C Cavalry Training Regiment, Redford Barracks 1940. Later CO Pack-Mule Transport Regiment. Father of Ian (above).

EBRINGTON, Lieutenant Viscount, Peter. Troop Leader. KIA 1942.
EDMISTON, Lieutenant Gordon, MC. Troop Leader.

FINDLAY, Lieutenant Colonel Sir Roland L. Bart. Squadron Leader. Wounded 1942.
FITZGEORGE PARKER, Captain T.B., MC, (Tim or Timmie). Troop Leader. Signals Officer.

GREY, Lieutenant C.R. (Bob). Troop Leader.
GREGORY, Captain R. (Bob). Posted from 8th Hussars as our first Technical Adjutant on mechanisation 1941.
GUINNESS, Major Humphrey M.P. Squadron Leader, 2I/C.
GUNN, Major H. John D., MC. Troop Leader. Signals Officer. Squadron Leader.

HALL, Captain Michael (Mike). Reinforcement from 4th/7th Dragoon Guards. Troop Leader.
HALSWELL, Major W., known as Peter. Squadron Leader. OC 'B' Echelon.
HANBURY, Major James. Troop Leader. Squadron 2I/C.
HICKS, Captain R.E. (Bob). Troop Leader. Technical Adjutant.
HOLLAND, Captain Sir Guy H., Bart. Troop Leader. Wounded 1942.
HOWARD, Lieutenant J. Roy. Troop Leader. KIA 1943.
HUTCHESON, Lieutenant W.J.S. Troop Leader. KIA 1943.

JOHNSTON, Captain J., MC, (Johnnie), RAMC. Regimental Medical Officer 1942–45.

LARCOM, Captain A. (Tony). Posted from Westminister Dragoons as Technical Adjutant 1944.
LEWIS, Colonel A.W.D., MC, (Alec). Troop Leader. RIO. CO 1957–59.
LYCETT, Major Michael H.L., CBE. Troop Leader. Squadron 2I/C.

MACLENNAN, The Rev. J.D., RAChD (Mac), known as Wee Mac and Tom Thumb. Regimental Padre 1942–46.
MAHONEY, Captain T.A., MC and Bar, (Tom). Troop Leader. Squadron 2I/C.
MARSHALL, Lieutenant Hilary. Troop Leader. Also known as 'Brenda' after a leading actress of the time.
MERCER, Lieutenant Andrew. Troop Leader.
MILBURN, Major Rupert L.E., (Ru). Troop Leader. Adjutant.
MILES, Captain Basil, RAMC. Regimental Medical Officer 1941–42. Wounded 1942.

PAGET, Major Peter W., MC. Squadron 2I/C. Squadron Leader. KIA 1944.
PARKIN, Lieutenant John. Troop Leader.

PEARS, Lieutenant J. Seymour. Troop Leader. KIA 1943.

PERKINS, Lieutenant J.A. Troop Leader. KIA 1944.

PLEWS, Lieutenant Graham R. Troop Leader. KIA 1943.

RADCLYFFE, Captain C.R. (Charlie). Troop Leader.

READMAN, Lieutenant Colonel A.G.J., DSO, (Tim). Squadron Leader. 2I/C. CO
1942–44 and 1948–49. Hon. Colonel 1968–71.

READMAN, Lieutenant Colonel Ian R., MC. Troop Leader. Wounded 1944.

REAY, Lieutenant H.M. Paul. Regimental Liaison Officer. Wounded 1944.

ROBINSON, Major E.R.W., MC (Ted or Ted Rob). Troop Leader. OC 'A' Echelon.
Squadron Leader.

ROBOROUGH, Major Lord, Massey. Squadron Leader.

SHELLEY, Captain Richard R. Reinforcement from 4th/7th Dragoon Guards. Troop
Leader. Adjutant.

STEWART, Lieutenant Colonel D.N., DSO, MC and Bar (Duggie). Squadron Leader.
CO 1945–47 and 1950–53.

SYMINGTON, Captain Denis. Troop Leader. Signals Officer.

TODD, Brigadier George H.N., MC. CO 1939–42. Honorary Colonel 1947–58.

TWISTLETON-WYKEHAM-FIENNES, Lieutenant Colonel Sir Ranulph, Bart., DSO.
Called 'Lugs' by everyone both in and out of the Regiment. CO 1942–43. Died of
wounds 1943.

WARRENDER, Colonel The Hon. John R., MC, later Lord Bruntisfield. Troop Leader.
Adjutant.

WILLIAMS, Major Sir Michael O., Bart., MC, also known as 'Mo' (his initials).
Squadron 2I/C. Squadron Leader.

Note: There were five 'Peters' serving together; so as to avoid confusion, they were
referred to, or known as:

Peter B – Borwick
Downie Bird – Downie
Peter Eb – Ebrington
Peter Has – Halswell
Peter Paj – Paget

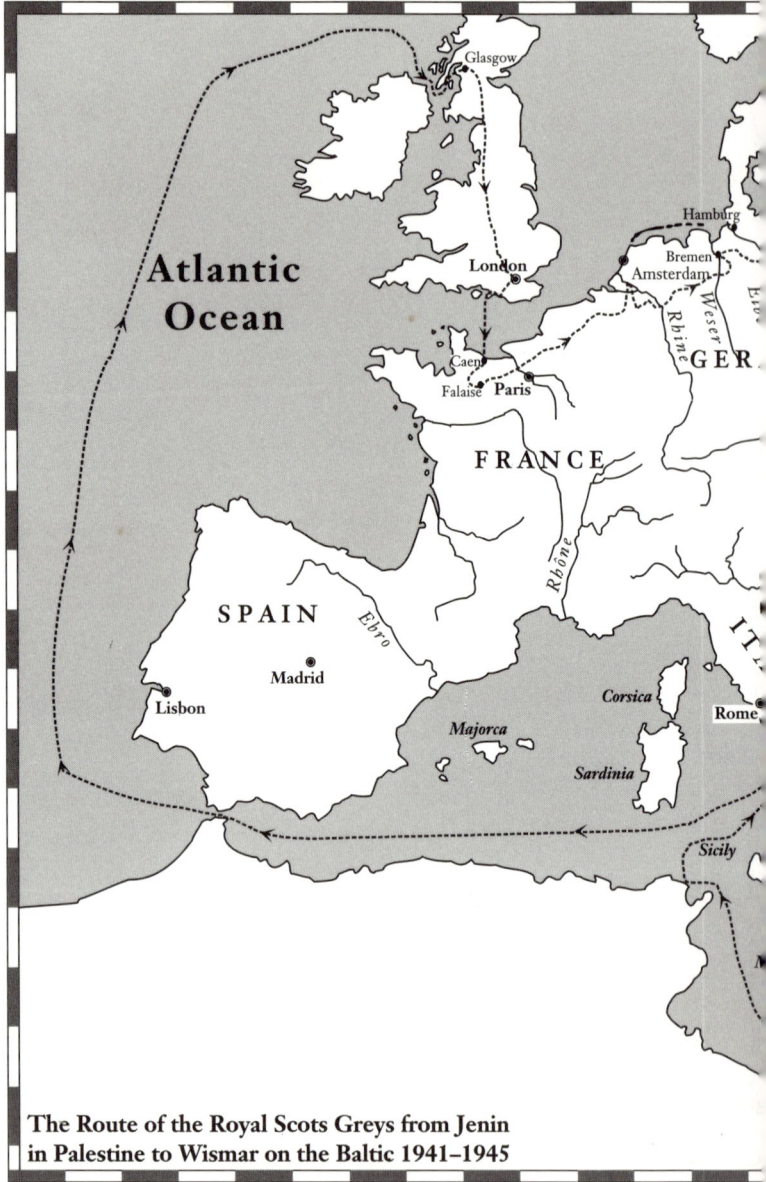

Atlantic
Ocean

Glasgow

Hamburg

Bremen
Amsterdam

London

GER

Caen

Falaise Paris

FRANCE

SPAIN

Madrid

Lisbon

Corsica

Rome

Majorca

Sardinia

IT

Sicily

The Route of the Royal Scots Greys from Jenin
in Palestine to Wismar on the Baltic 1941–1945